TENNIS
PLAY SMARTER NOT HARDER II

Your On-Court Tennis Coach

CURLY DAVIS

Copyright © 2012. Curly Davis
All rights reserved.

ISBN: 1478238674
ISBN-13: 9781478238676

TABLE OF CONTENT

Acknowledgments xi

Chapter I – Curl's Pearls 1
   a. Psychology
      i. First Things First 1
      ii. Good or Bad Thought, Go With Your
         First Thought 2
      iii. Stroke Instead of Choke 3
      iv. If You're Wrong, Be Long 4
   b. Forehand
      i. The Power Triangle 5
      ii. Don't Take Your Racket Back 5
      iii. One "L" of a Forehand 9
      iv. Wave Good-bye to Your High Forehand Problems . 14
      v. Progressive Forehand Approach Shot Footwork . . . 19
      vi. Rip from the Hip 21
   c. Backhand
      i. S.E.T. 22
      ii. Turn, Tuck, and Swing Up 23
      iii. Throw a Frisbee 24
      iv. High Backhand Smash—If You Have to...
         Here's How To 24
   d. Volleys
      i. Half Volleys—If You Have to...Here's How To . . . 26
      ii. Three Ways to Keep from Swinging Too
         BIG on your Volleys 28
         A. Banning Too Much Swing on Your Volleys . 28
         B. Point Your Finger at Your Volley Problems 29
         C. Elbows In 29

- iii. Hit Through the Court, Not To the Court 29
- iv. Stick, Stop, and Stomp 30
- v. Extend and Bend 31
- vi. Low Go, High Good-Bye 32

e. Serve
  - i. The Serve should be a Roller Coaster Ride 34
  - ii. Thrust and Bust 35
  - iii. Whip Your Opponent with a Timely Serve 36
  - iv. Let's Have a Toast for a Better Serve Toss 36
  - v. Pronate to Generate 37
  - vi. Jump Through Hoops! 38

f. Return of Serve
  - i. First Serve, Make Them Play; Second Serve, Make Them Pay 40
  - ii. One, Two, Hop, and Hit 41
  - iii. Stay Back on Flat, Move In on Spin 42

g. Court Coverage
  - i. Hit and Get 43
  - ii. Feet Move—Swing Smooth 44
  - iii. Footwork—Adjustment Steps Followed by a Balance Step 45
  - iv. Rip and Run 45
  - v. Dash and Cash 46
  - vi. Shoot and Scoot 46
  - vii. Rush and Crush 46
  - viii. Smash and Crash 46
  - ix. Split Step, Not Split Stop 46
  - x. Split Step—It's When, Not Where 47
  - xi. Lobs…Don't Have to Be a Four-Letter Word 47
  - xii. Absorbing Depth 50

h. Spins and Strokes
  - i. Slice—the 3-Ds 51
  - ii. Slice is Nice but Topspin Wins 56
  - iii. Topspin…Accelerate, Abbreviate, Exaggerate 58
  - iv. Erase the Space 59

		v. Less is More 60

       v.   Less is More 60
      vi.   Less is Best...................................... 61
     vii.   If Your Strokes Fail Ya, Hit Australia 61
    viii.   In Tennis, "But" is the Rule, Not the Exception ... 62
      ix.   The K.I.S. Swing—Keep It Simple.............. 67
       x.   Feel or Touch 69
      xi.   I Have to Hand it to You—Quick Hands,
           Fast Hands, Soft Hands 72
     xii.   Framing Contact 73
 i. Anticipation
       i.   Know What Area You're In,
          Know What Shot to Select, ... 74
      ii.   Approach Shots—You Get or You Give 77
     iii.   When They're Stretching, You're Fetching....... 78
     iv.   See Their Buns, You Run 79
      v.   If They Don't Show It, Then You Don't Know It .. 80
     vi.   What You See is What You Get 81
 j. Tactics
       i.   Hitting the Right Shot to the Right Spot........ 83
      ii.   Three to Five to Stay Alive 84
     iii.   Passing Shot Patterns—Dip and Rip 86
     iv.   Passing Shots Patterns—Dump and Jump 87
      v.   Passing Shot Patterns—High and Low 87
     vi.   Rules that Apply to Any Sport 88
          A.   If It Ain't Broke; Don't Fix It 88
          B.   Dance With Who Brung Ya 88
          C.   If You're Losin'...Start Cruisin'........... 88
     vii.   Take the Ball on the Rise and Give
          Them a Surprise 89
    viii.   Don't Retreat, Take the Heat 90
 k. Doubles Teamwork
       i.   Down the Middle Solves the Riddle 90
      ii.   Sliding and Deciding 91
     iii.   Poaching – Fake It Till You Make It............ 92
     iv.   Poaching – Disguise to Neutralize 94

      v. Poaching – Hit the Way You Move,
          Then Move the Way You Hit 94
     vi. Position without Possession 95
   vii. Hug and Hover 96

Chapter II – Diagnosing Weaknesses 99
   a. Grips…Know Their Soft Spots 100
   b. Stroke Styles and Where to Attack 104
   c. Stroke Styles 107
   d. Playing Styles – Rock, Scissors, or Paper? 109
   e. Scouting Report 114

Chapter III – Applying Pressure 117
   a. Pace 118
   b. Power 119
   c. Spin 120
   d. Placement 122
   e. Position 124

Chapter IV – Tricks of the Trade 127
   a. Trick #1—When You Break a String During the Point . . 127
   b. Trick #1A—When you break a string during a point
      and can't get to the net 128
   c. Trick #1B—When your opponent breaks a string 128
   d. Trick #1C 128
   e. Trick #2—Net Cord? Racket Up! 129
   f. Trick #3—Wind Wisdom: Making the Wind
      Your Friend 129
   g. Spin 130
   h. Position 130
   i. Cross-Court Winds 131
   j. Serve 131
   k. Shot Selections 132
   l. Trick #4—Heavy Weather Conditions 132
   m. Trick #5—What to Choose When You Win the Toss 134

n. Trick #6—Miss-hits? Hit Them! 136
o. Trick #7—Drop Shots: Focus, Frantic, or Fatigue? 136
p. Trick #8—Put-Aways and Why They Get Away 137
q. Trick #9—Rules of Opposing Styles.................. 138
r. Trick #10—Breaking Serve, Think First and Third 140
s. Trick #10 – It's Not a Break Until You Hold 142
t. Trick #10a—0–0 is the best time to be broken......... 142
u. Trick #11—Rain Delays and How to Respond 143
v. Trick #12—Regripping? A Penny for Your Thoughts.... 146

Chapter V – Curlyisms 149
a. Great Shots Win Points, Good Shots Win Matches...... 149
b. Tennis Players Are a Bunch of Losers 150
c. Progress Today Determines Tomorrow's Achievements... 150
d. Expect with Respect................................ 151
e. Failure is an Event...Not a Person 151
f. Learning Occurs When... 152
g. Don't Let What's Going Wrong Get in the
   Way of What's Going Right........................ 152
h. Points are Won and Lost Well Before They're
   Won or Lost 153
i. Go Through the Strength to Open Up the Weakness 154
j. Winning Breeds Complacency 154
k. You Get What You Give 155
l. It's Not What You Did Wrong; It's What Your
   Opponent Did Right 156
m. Big Points Don't Mean You Have to Hit Big Shots...... 157
n. Are There Big Points in Tennis?..................... 158
o. A Questionable Call Should Cost Only One Point 158
p. Cheating is Fleeting 159
q. Titles—If You're Not Enough without Them
   Then You Won't be Enough with Them 159
r. Will Beats Skill 160

About the Author 163

"This book is dedicated to my loving parents, both have passed, who gave me tough love when needed and encouragement when needed. I am a very fortunate person to have them as my parents."

Acknowledgments

As in my first book, I want to thank everyone whom I have the pleasure to know and learn from. I've learned so much from so many teaching professionals and hope to learn more. But also, as in my first book, I must thank some important people in my life.

First, my family—my father, who introduced me to the sport of tennis and a way of touching lives. My mother, who encouraged me to place my thoughts on paper; this started my writing. Both parents have passed and I miss their daily guidance and wisdom. My brother Alfie and his family, who show the steadfastness in the family unit; he has been a rock!

To Don Kaiser, who is always present in my teaching. Every teaching pro should be so fortunate as to have such a mentor. He's the one person who opened my mind to looking for everyday actions and correlating them into teaching tennis.

To my friends who are pictured in the book; Don Paitrick, a GREAT teaching pro; Harry Pino, knows more about court movement and preparation than anyone I know; Ryan Pinosky, a student of mine and fine young gentleman; Bill Beverly, brings enthusiasm to his lessons and we all know, "enthusiasm is contagious"; Trish and Dwaine Gullett, they have helped in many ways to bring about this book along with appearing in this book; John Nigro, he's the best at motivating his students to want to perform well for him.

Finally and most important to me, the people who taught me life happens and should be lived "one day at a time."

CHAPTER 1

Curl's Pearls

Psychology

First Things First

Many tennis players worry about their opponent and where to hit the ball, but in reality, if they have a concern it should be with the three problems that face them when they are on the court.

1. *Getting the ball over the net*—The myth is that to be good you must be able to hit low and hard, and tennis players tend to attempt to aim the ball low and to hit it hard. In actuality, as long as your opponent is back at the baseline, feel free to hit the ball three to five feet* above the net. You will find that by aiming higher over the net, not only do you eliminate any net mistakes, your ball will land deeper in your opponent's court. Height gives depth.

2. *Getting the ball in the lines*—It takes ability and courage from your opponent when you hit the ball close to the lines. READ THAT STATEMENT AGAIN. Your opponent needs the ability to recognize that a ball that is going to be out and then the courage to tell you something that you don't want to hear—OUT! How many points have you given your opponent because you weren't sure where it landed? If you

play by the rules—which state that when in doubt you must give the benefit to your opponent— the answer is "too many." Another question: How many times have you given points to opponents because they hit it into the net? *Never!*

3. *Your opponent*—If you were to rate your opponent's ability on a scale from one to ten (one being the worst), their ability has to be a one if you hit the ball into the net. I'd give them a one for their ability to stand and watch.

In summary, first things first. Don't worry about your opponent if you can't get it in, and don't worry about getting it in if you can't get it over the net.

Psychology

Good or Bad Thought, Go with Your First Thought

Has this situation ever happened to you? You are about to strike the ball. At the last moment you change your mind about to where to place the shot, and the result is a mistake. Of course it has! It has happened to all tennis players. But why does it happen? I have found that changing your mind is a result of one or all of three things: 1) too many options, 2) noticing your opponent's movement to the area where you were going to place the ball, and 3) realizing at the last moment you made a bad shot selection.

Let's look at each reason. First, too many options—especially when you have an easy shot. For example, maybe your first thought was to drop shot the ball, but then you decide to drive the ball instead. As a result, you make the mistake of hitting the ball long.

Second, seeing your opponent move causes you to change your mind, because you know that your opponent is moving toward where you were directing your shot. You are making a mistake by taking your eyes off the ball. In fact, you may want to remember the effect that movement had on *you* the next time your opponent has an easy shot. Any move you make may cause them to change their mind and make a mistake.

Third, you are about to strike the ball when you realize that it is not the correct shot selection. You change your mind to the correct shot and once again you are making a mistake. Even if it is a bad selection, you have a better prospect of executing the proper stroke at that moment giving you greater probability to win the point.

The answer in preventing a last-minute change of mind is in the title: *good thought or bad thought, go with your first thought.* Even if your opponent is moving to where you are hitting the ball, they haven't won the point; all they did was guess correctly. Bad thoughts still can turn out better than changing your mind.

Psychology

Stroke Instead of Choke

Don't hit the ball into the net. Don't hit the ball long. Don't hit the ball right back to your opponent! Does that sound like another one of those conversations going on inside your head during a match? It happens to every one of us and, invariably, when we say *don't*, unfortunately we *do*. You are setting yourself up to choke!

In tight situations, we should be thinking positive thoughts. As tennis players, we always do better when we reinforce the positive. Next time negative thoughts start to invade your head, tell yourself what you *want* to do with the stroke instead of what you *don't* want to do.

In addition to thinking positive, try to control your breathing. You may notice that right after a key point, most pros will take a little more time and take a deep breath before the start of the next point to ensure that they are completely relaxed. Once your muscles are relaxed, you will find that you will be able to stroke the ball instead of choke.

Psychology

If You're Wrong, Be Long

In tennis, there are two mistakes players can make: 1) hitting into the net and, 2) hitting out (long or wide). Of the two, I would rather see a player hit long instead of into the net.

Why do I say that? To hit the ball into the net, you could have several technical flaws in your stroke resulting in the netted ball. Conversely, if you hit the ball long, you must be doing something technically correct with your strokes to have it go that far.

Furthermore, if the ball goes into the net, your opponent will not have an opportunity to give you the benefit of the doubt on the call, but if your ball lands close to the baseline or sideline, and they aren't sure if it landed in or out, they are supposed to give you the benefit of the doubt. Finally, as a coach, when I see a stroke go into the net, especially a second serve, I think that the player may be tightening up a bit, and tightening up scares coaches because it affects every stroke in an adverse way. So, *if you're going to be wrong, be long.*

Forehand

The Power Triangle

It has been established that when you hit a ground stroke, *hand is control and body is power.* Combine the two, and you maximize control and power.

To hit a forehand, imagine a triangle connecting the hand, hip, and shoulder. To prepare for an open stance forehand, the first move is to turn the shoulders as the body coils. Releasing the power into the shot comes from uncoiling by throwing the hip and shoulder into the stroke as the hand determines the direction. It's a three-apart action performed in unison, best visualized as three parts working together. When the hand, hip, and shoulder function as a unit, power and control will result every time.

Forehand

Don't Take Your Racket Back!
The Advantages of the Intermediate Racket Position

In teaching the forehand stroke, every tennis instructor repeatedly says to players, "Take your racket back sooner." What the instructor is really asking the player to do is to sweep the racket straight back at slightly below waist level, while aligning the forward foot with the selected target, This prepares the player for a low-to-high hit from a closed stance. It has worked for years for some pretty remarkable players, but times change, and improvements are found even in the game of tennis.

There are several difficulties with the closed-stance method of straight-back racket preparation.

1. *It impedes the racket head speed into the shot.* Extending the racket fully backward brings it to a momentary waiting position and loses the fluid motion of the backswing, which would contribute to the accelerated forward movement needed for maximum power.

2. *Flexibility when making the shot is limited.* Adjusting to the high-kicking, topspin-hit ball and the low, sliced shot from a waist-level straight takeaway requires unusual quickness to properly meet the ball and produce the desired result in today's faster game.

CURL'S PEARLS

3. *Court coverage is reduced by straight-back preparation.* Better tennis players run with their arms away from their sides in a pumping motion, like a sprinter, then explode into the shot from a naturally coiled body. This is nearly impossible with the racket extended behind you.

In contradiction to the classic forehand closed stance, today's recommendation is intermediate racket position. IRP can be accomplished in two ways. Simply rotating the hips and shoulders will position the racket head at eye level, close to the body, in the first movement for an attacking, inside-out swing.

From this ready start, the approaching ball is tracked with the racket for height of bounce. You finish the combined backward-and-forward stroke by dropping the racket head under the ball's contact point and following through. Watch today's players hit a forehand for a prime example of this style.

A second IRP method is to first rotate the hips and shoulders but then let the elbow lead the racket into the desired position for an attacking swing.

A loose shoulder is required for the shoulder–elbow–racket combination to then move back close to the body and under the ball for the low-to-high finish. Once you've seen several of the top touring professionals hit with this forehand take back, you will see the benefits.

With both of these IRP preparations, the initial rotation is essential. The power is generated by reversing the rotation of the hips and shoulders and leading the racket head into meeting and following through the ball. With either of the IRP starts, by reversing the rotation the racket is drawn or pulled forcibly through the shot setup and then finished with a wraparound motion. And you will want the back leg to come around into the stroke, adding to it the lower-body power and finishing in a ready stance for the next shot.

Pictures above also show the proper open-stance foot position with the weight-loaded back foot inside the oncoming ball line, which maximizes the hip and shoulder thrust.

Practice IRP and you will hit with more power and spin and more readily return shots of different heights that come from your opponents.

Forehand

One "L" of a Forehand

A number of years ago, forehand was essentially a straight arm-swing, a movement similar to a door swinging open and closed. The arm was "hinged" at the shoulder and remained relatively straight throughout the swing. Those days are gone. Players are finding different, more powerful ways to hit the forehand. The most common is a throwing motion, named a "chain-reaction motion." This chain-reaction sequence is linked together by different parts of the arm forming the letter L. When the L's are performed with proper timing, power and precision are greatly enhanced. So you know how to incorporate the "L's" in your game, let's examine them.

1. *The backswing "L"* - —The racket moves to an *intermediate racket position* (IRP). Shown are two IRP positions. In the first picture, the arm is going up with the striking side of the racket surface facing out. The second IRP has the elbow lifting as it is drawn back. Both IRP backswings form an "L" while in this position, allowing you the flexibility to adjust to different height contact points. This "L" also contributes to an accelerated arm action to facilitate more topspin and speed on the shot.

CURL'S PEARLS

2. *The "L" drop*—The hand drops the racket head *below* and *behind* the hand. Starting the hand below the ball assures a lifting action to the stroke and, with the hand *preceding* the racket, positions the hand and wrist for more power on the ball by using articular flexibility—the elasticity of the wrist joint—to enable the flexibility of the wrist to throw the racket face behind the ball.

3. *The contact "L"*—The forearm and wrist form the "L" this is to give the hand stability and support needed at impact. Otherwise, a straight arm returning a hard-hit ball will falter under the force of the collision.

4. *The "L" follow-through*—First, we ought to realize that follow-through and finish are two different segments of the swing. The follow-through is the moment after impact. In addition, you are either following through forward or more vertically; forward is for penetration and a vertical swing is for more spin. The deciding factor is tactical intent. With a vertical swing, the forearm and bicep are forming the "L". This lifts the ball and gives it more spin.

CURL'S PEARLS

5. *The L finish*—When you finish the stroke, the racket wraps around the neck, concluding over the non-dominant shoulder. This L, formed with the wrist and forearm, allows the body to come to a unobstructed finish.

TENNIS: PLAY SMARTER NOT HARDER II

Now that you know how to hit the "L" out of the forehand, take the "L"-evator to the top of the rankings.

Forehand

Wave Good-bye to Your High Forehand Problems

Many players have trouble with a high-bouncing forehand ball—a ball chest high and above. The most common reaction is to retreat far enough to allow the ball to drop to waist level then make the basic low-to-high stroke. This is acceptable, but there are situations where neither time nor tactical intent makes it an advantage to retreat. An alternative must then be found. When hitting a high ball consider five recommended adjustments:

1. *Adopt a Western grip:* They position the wrist beneath the racket handle, creating a stronger forearm. A weak arm is one of the principal problems of players attempting to respond to a high ball. The proper grip also promotes the correct wrist use. "What? Use my wrist?" Yes! There is wrist use in tennis! It's a vertical wrist (up and down) *not* a horizontal

CURL'S PEARLS

wrist ("slapping motion"). The vertical wrist use allows the arm, and racket face, to move freely up and then across the back of the ball. The laws of physics dictate that a ball, no matter the height of contact, must leave the racket traveling up when hit from the baseline area, in order to clear the net. "But if I hit up, won't the ball go long?" Not necessarily. The ball finds the court in one of two ways—by gravity or spin. If you make contact behind the ball and then move the racket face up across the ball, it will impart the desired spin to direct the ball into the opponent's court. In short, more spin prevents the shot going long.

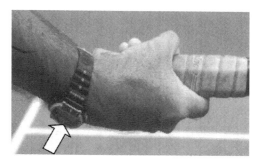

Note watch face: The semi-western or western grips are the choice for the high bouncing ball.

2. *Use the intermediate racket position:* This preparation will result in sending the ball long —Whether you're backing up and letting the ball drop or taking the ball higher and earlier, the intermediate racket position is essential to your success in handling a high ball. The IRP responds to the high contact point the best of all the takeaways, because it lines the racket up at the same level as the anticipated contact. The racket adjusts more easily in every contact zone with the principle of "track it with your racket," which means following or tracking the ball as it is coming to you.

Note in the "YES" picture, the racquet face "tracks (follows) the ball so it is on the same level as the anticipated contact point. The "NO" picture shows the racquet starting low, with the front shoulder angling up.

3. *Employ an open stance*: There is a semi-open stance, and a full-open stance. Both are correct and effective, with one of the two being recommended for most forehand shots, especially for a high ball. It allows the non-racket side to "clear out" during the swing for an unrestricted finish. The arm can then move freely away from the body in following through over the shoulder on the non-racket side. The open stance also allows for the lower body (hips) to rotate unimpeded into the stroke, giving more power to the shot.

4. *Move the racket arm in a waving motion* —When waving to someone, note how the wrist is laid back, placing the palm outward, (finger tips upward), the forearm and hand moving back and forth. This movement is the same motion as the swing for a high forehand. The racket goes across the back of the ball, spinning it deep into the other court. A common error is trying to make contact rolling the arm over the ball, resulting in a downward flight into the net.

5. *Show your butt...of the racket*—A common mistake is to finish a high forehand stroke with the racket down and across the body. This will cause the ball to drop quickly into the net or land shallow on the other side. For the desired depth, finish with the butt of the racket pointing at the opponent's court. This will assure a high finish that sends the ball back deep and fast.

Good-bye high forehand problems...hello better tennis.

Forehand

Progressive Forehand Approach Shot Footwork

Previously, power and precision are not words that have gone together in tennis. However, in today's game, the balls are struck with unbelievable accuracy and with incredible power from everywhere on the court. One area is in the attacking (approach shot) zone of the court, particularly on the forehand side. No longer is the tactical intent of the forehand approach shot limited to setting up the volley winner. *The forehand approach* is *the winning shot!* How are the pros hitting that stroke with so much power? When we investigate more closely, we observe the coordination between the body and the arm delivering the power in the shot—a throwing or launching of the body, as the racket is thrown against the ball. What facilitates the launching are three footwork methods to the forehand approach, all of which I encourage you to try; one of them is appropriate for your game. (This article assumes the reader is right-handed.)

Extension jump—You approach the ball in a conventional style, left foot forward (frame a), followed by extending (jumping) off the left foot (frame b), and landing on the left foot (frame c). This jump throws the body weight into the stroke, creating more power while allowing the arm to remain as the control source. This footwork is effective for handling the high bouncing balls, chest height or higher in a mid-court zone.

Extension rotation —This is a more conventional approach to adding more power into the approach shot, by allowing the hips to "fire into" the ball, creating more angular momentum (body rotation) in the shot. You use the traditional footwork, left foot in front, and then as the racket starts forward, you bring your right foot forward, a *hand-through–hips- through* action. You will find it easier to adapt this to your game, since it is so similar to the conventional approach, allowing for an easier transition towards the net. Finally, this footwork manages the medium height—chest height to knee height—bouncing balls effectively.

Extension thrust —This is the newest style on the forehand approach and possibly the most difficult to coordinate. It is performed regularly when the ball you're attacking is to the outside third of the court. The dominant side foot (right foot shown in frame a) is in front of the non-dominant foot and then as the racket comes forward to meet the ball, the non-dominate foot is propelled, (thrust) forward towards the ball. This footwork makes it easier to "redirect" a cross-court ball down-the-line also is effective on all height balls, and on return of serves.

Forehand

Rip from the Hip

In today's game the forehand ground stroke and the serve are the two most consistent power strokes in the game. Where are the pros are getting their power? Racket technology is one way, strength training is another, but the answer that you can immediately incorporate into your game is that players are throwing their dominant side hip into the stroke.

This hip rotation starts when the dominant side foot goes at an angle to the net; then the swing starts forward, and the right knee (assuming you're right-handed) rotates counterclockwise, thrusting the hip out and resulting in the upper body and racket arm being thrown at the ball.

To practice this rotation of the hips, place a five- to ten-pound medicine ball right in front of your stomach, then shift the ball—first to your left side, then to your right side. Notice how your hips are rotating while doing this? Notice how your knees are rotating to allow the "trunk rotation"?

Now that you have the feel of the body rotation, next time on the forehand *let it rip from the hip!*

Backhand

S.E.T. -

When you prepare to hit a backhand, you have three checks points to make sure the preparation is correct, S.E.T.—that's an acronym for Shoulder, Elbow, and Thumb.

Shoulder—the racket shoulder should go back and touch the chin. This is to make sure you have your body ready to rotate into the stroke.

Elbow—the elbow should go back in, close to the bellybutton. Keeping the elbow close to the body ensure that you're going to swing from the shoulder. If you start with the elbow too far away from the body, you'll push or poke at the ball, using only the forearm to swing at the ball.

Thumb—the right thumb (left thumb, if you're left-handed) should go back and touch the left hip (or right hip, if you're left handed). The thumb against the hip makes certain that your swing goes from low to high. This helps lift the ball over the net.

Backhand

Turn, Tuck, and Swing Up

When you see a ball coming to your backhand there are three points of reference to recall in preparation of the backhand:

Turn—your right shoulder, (if right-handed, left shoulder if you're left-handed) back to where it makes contact with your chin. This check-point makes sure that you have the proper shoulder rotation in readiness for the stroke.

Tuck—your right elbow (if right-handed, left elbow if left-handed) into your bellybutton. This tucking of the elbow will ensure that there is no space between the elbow and the body as you prepare for the stroke. If you do have a gap between the elbow and the stomach, your swing will result in a jabbing or pushing stroke, with the result being loss of power and depth on the shot.

Swing up—This will ensure a lifting action to your swing, which will help elevate the ball over the net, while making sure your head is still and will come up with the follow-through.

Backhand

Throw a Frisbee

If you have ever thrown a Frisbee before, whether you were successful or not makes no difference. It's the motion of throwing a Frisbee that I want you to emulate.

When throwing a Frisbee and when hitting a backhand:

1. You turn the shoulders,

2. Your arm starts close to the body,

3. Your hand is low by the hip, and

4. You release the arm out to your target.

Practice your backhand by throwing a Frisbee.

Backhand

High Backhand Smash—If You Have to...Here's How To

We all dread those lobs that are over the backhand side. What do we do with them? Let them bounce? Run around them? Hit them as a high backhand?

The first option is to always attempt to run around and hit an overhead, but that will be determined if the lob is high enough to afford you the time to back around it to hit an overhead. If time does not allow, you must find other alternatives. One such option is the high backhand smash!

CURL'S PEARLS

First you must realize that the backhand smash is one of the hardest strokes to control. Why? In tennis, *body is power, arm is control.* The body gives you the power on swings by stepping in and rotating into the strokes. The arm gives you the control by positioning the racket face in the direction you intend for the shot to travel. With this understanding, you can observe a high backhand smash and see that the body usually is moving away from (not able to step into) the intended direction, as the player attempts to get into position to strike the ball. Furthermore, the higher the contact point, the less the lower body can assist in delivering power to the stroke. That explains why there's no power on the high backhand. With the body not able to deliver the power, then the arm must bear dual responsibilities, control and power, and one suffers—usually control.

The stroke—The racket shoulder turns and tucks itself under the chin. This ensures the correct shoulder rotation and shoulder position. By raising the arm up, this aligns the racket arm for the anticipated contact.

Shoulder alignment—Be aware the racket, and thus the ball, will follow the shoulder alignment. When you have attempted high backhands in the past, the ball may have gone wide of the court; the shoulder alignment was the cause.

Footwork—When recognizing the lob, first turn getting sideways to the net. Then make a crossover run for the ball, right foot going in front of left. Once you are in the location you want, jump and then snap the arm.

Placement—Since power is difficult to generate on the high backhand, focus on placement. Let your right shoulder (if right handed) direct the ball to the angles. The racket face should make contact with the outside of the ball, and then the racket follows your shoulder. To generate some power and placement, try reverse pronation.

Reverse pronation—You have heard about pronation on the serve. In this scenario, you want *reverse* pronation to help direct (turn) the arm—and thus the racket face—to the target area, preventing the racket from following your shoulder alignment. This also gives the snap (power) to the stroke. Your arm will stop abruptly when it gets about level with the shoulder, snapping the arm through point of contact in a whip motion.

Volleys

Half Volleys—If You Have to...Here's How To

The half-volley is a stroke you mostly hit when approaching the net. In these circumstances, your opponent has returned a ball at your feet and you don't have time to move in and take it out of the air because it's dropping too fast. Typically you'll back-up to try and let the ball bounce giving yourself more time to make the shot. By doing this, however, the ball will bounce at an angle that will make it more difficult, rather than less. Also, with your body backing up, the ball will come off your racket with a high trajectory, moving into the opponent's court for an easy put-away.

When hitting a half volley, basics to success are:

1. *The lower the ball contact, the wider our stance should be.* This wider stance lowers the center of gravity, resulting in better balance, and it keeps the body moving forward. The wider stance also makes for a longer hitting zone.

2. *Keep moving forward.* A common mistake players make is to stop their forward movement. This reduces power on the stroke and makes recovery for the next shot more difficult.

3. *Use a limited stroke.* Use little or no backswing and a short follow-through. Since the ball is bouncing right in front of you, you don't have time for the big backswing, and a big follow-through will send the ball out of the court. Place a ball in your arm-pit on your dominate side with your racket. Have someone throw a ball at your feet. Practice hitting without dropping the ball from your arm-pit. This will give you the feeling of a "limited swing."

4. *Placement.* The placement of your half volley should be deep to a corner so your opponent has to move left or right to get to your shot. Do *not* try to hit this shot with power. This is a touch shot, not a power shot.

The half volley is a stroke you should practice so you feel confident in hitting it, but is not a stroke that is part of the overall strategy to win a match. You have never heard a touring pro say, "My strategy was to serve and half-volley my opponent off the court"!

Volleys

Three Ways to Keep from Swinging Too BIG on Your Volleys

1. *Banning too much swing on your volley.* Are you tired of hearing your tennis instructor telling you, "Stop swinging on your volleys"? This trick will help. The problem of swinging too much may be caused by the non-dominant hand moving away from the body. You'll find the other arm will do the same, as we see in the picture below. In short, "for every action there is an equal and opposite reaction." The trick is place your hands through a headband, This will force the arms to move together, so that the shoulders down to the hips move as a unit (approximately a sixty-degree turn), and it isn't possible for the arms to move away from the body. Try this and your volley will be headed in the correct direction.

2. *Point your finger at your volley problems.* If you are a little self-conscious and don't want to place your hands through a headband, you can try a different approach with the same result. To cut down on your swing, take your non-dominant index finger and place it on the wrist of your dominant arm. Have someone feed balls to you. Keep your index finger on your wrist as you hit the ball. This will keep your dominant arm from swinging too much.

3. *Elbows In.* The final approach is to take your non-dominant arm and place it under the elbow of the dominant arm. Then have someone feed balls to you, this will restrict the dominant arm from moving away from the body.

All three of these suggestions will make you feel the reduced arm swing that we are seeking. If not...then the last-ditch effort to stop you from swinging on your volleys is to take the handcuffs out of the dresser drawer and place them on your wrist!

Volleys

Hit Through the Court, Not To the Court

What is meant by hitting *through* the court? Your volley should bounce once in the court and then penetrate the baseline or sidelines, as seen in the photo. Use the baseline as a yardstick to measure whether you are hitting through on your volleys. If your volley bounces once in the court and then shoot over the baseline (or the sidelines), it's deep or wide enough to create problems for your opponent.

When players hit the volley, all too frequently they play it safe and hit the ball *to* the open court instead of *through* the open court, as seen below. The problem with playing your volley to the court—in other words, too safely—is that it allows your opponent time to recover, reach your volley, and have another opportunity at a passing shot.

Have your volley exit the baseline or sideline, and your opponent will exit the tournament.

Volleys

Stick, Stop, and Stomp

In "Less is Best" (see *Curl's Pearls*), I talk about a more compact volley motion. In other words, the less swing you have, the fewer things that can go wrong, which results in the best volley you're going to hit.

CURL'S PEARLS

Keeping "less is best" in mind, there are but three components to a better volley:

1. *Stick* the racket up in front of the on-coming ball and stick it hard,

2. *Stop* after you hit the ball. Stop your swing; this will make the ball jump off the racket,

3. *Stomp* as you are making contact with the ball. Stomp your foot, and that will put your body behind the volley.

Low Volleys

Extend and Bend

When we approach the net, many times we get a difficult low volley to handle. Our first reaction is to back up and allow the ball to bounce; or maybe we handle it by not making a decision and just reaching for the ball with our upper body,

The rule of handling low volleys is simple: *extend and bend*. First, you make a decision to take the ball before it bounces, and then you extend out to the oncoming low volley with your left leg,

This widening of your base will lower your center of gravity, consequently giving you better balance during the stroke. Next you bend your knees low to the ball, particularly the back knee, which needs to bend low to the ground. Bending the back knee will ensure that you have your back straight, resulting in a perpendicular racket face. Finally, keep the racket head slightly above hand level, making for a longer hitting zone. The response of the ball coming off your racket will be a lower, more desirable trajectory.

Volleys

Low Go, High Good-Bye

You are playing doubles, and you are at the net at the net, ready to volley a ball. Your opponents are in the one-up–one-back formation. What are your best shot selections? The answer is found in the height of your contact point. If it's low, go; if it's high, good-bye! Or you can think of it this way: low hit the ball *to* the baseline player, if the ball is high, hit *through* the net player.

To illustrate *if it's low...go*: If the ball is low (below the net), you want to avoid the opposing net players because they will take that low volley that you just hit up and smash it for a winner. You want to take the low volley and direct it back to the player who is deeper in the court. That player might attempt another passing shot, but their chances are slim of hitting a winner.

If the ball is high...*good-bye* If the ball is above the net at contact, then you want to send the ball into the area of the net opponent. That player will have less reaction time since you are at such close range. Most often, they will try to avoid the ball rather than try and get it back. So...hit a high ball for a winner.

A word of caution: You need to base your shot decision on the height of your contact point, not on the height of the ball as it crosses the net. The ball can be high above the net as it crosses, but if you don't get to the ball until it has dropped well below the net, it can make a huge difference. The wrong "read" and you choose the wrong shot placement—and your opponents are winning the points.

Serve

The Serve should be a Roller Coaster Ride – Slow Start to a Fast Finish

Much too often, players will start their serve swing too fast just to have to slow down their swing to allow the ball toss to catch up with the rest of the swing—a fast start resulting in a slow finish, with the outcome being a "ride" without much exhilaration.

Can you remember your last roller coaster ride? It started slow and built up to a powerful acceleration; then we fell from the top of the ride.

The serve should be like that roller coaster ride, a very slow start with the focus on toss placement. Then, as you get to the top of the ride (the swing), the speed increases to a fast finish.

A slow start, fast finish will result in a thrill ride you won't forget and will want to ride again.

Serve

Thrust and Bust

When serving, many players just use their arms to generate power. What they fail to recognize is that the real power comes from the ground up. Your body must push off the ground to launch into the ball. This is called "ground-resistance force." To produce more power, you must use your body correctly.

Thrust up to the ball. To do this more effectively, you must flex your knees at the same time your hands goes up—one to toss the ball and the other to start the swing—an "up with the hands, down with the legs" motion. Now your body is loaded up to use the ground to thrust up toward the ball. Watch a basketball player prepare to get a rebound. Notice how he flexes his legs in preparation to launch his body toward the ball.

Bust the ball. The service swing should start in a slow, relaxed, rhythmic motion. As the swing gets to the top of its motion behind the back, the legs start driving the body up into the ball as the swing accelerates into it—a busting of the ball.

Serve

Whip Your Opponent with a Timely Serve

The phrase "wrist snap," used when describing the serve motion, is often misinterpreted by players. Many players hear "wrist snap" and translate it into stopping the arm motion at the top of the swing and then snapping the wrist through the rest of the swing and ending up with a "waving motion."

Instead, visualize the snapping action of the arm and shoulder when using a whip. To use a whip, your shoulder moves quickly and then stops abruptly creating a snapping action with the arm and out to the whip. While the shoulder and arm produce a snapping action, the forearm is rotating forward and in the same motion as if someone asked you "What time is it?" Your forearm turns out and your palm is down as if to roll your watch face towards you to see the time.

To whip up your opponent and have your serve clocked at a greater speed, have your arm snap in a timely manner.

Serve

Let's Have a Toast for a Better Serve Toss

Most tennis players share the same problem on the serve: an inconsistent ball toss. In all of my years of teaching, I've never seen a consistent serve with an inconsistent ball toss. The toss is too far in front, too far behind, too far left, too far right. The origin of the erratic ball toss seems to be the bending or hingeing of the wrist or forearm.

To prevent the wrist and forearm from controlling the toss, think of the ball as a glass of water. Note the hand position is to the side of the glass, not beneath as frequently positioned. Placing the hand to the side of the ball, positioning the hand where it restricts unwanted wrist action, and make a lifting movement as if raising a glass in a toast.

When toasting with your service, you can drink up the praises you'll receive with a consistent serve.

Serve

Pronate to Generate

Pronation has been discussed and written about by many, but what is it? Webster's Dictionary defines pronation as "the turning outward and downward of the palm of the hand."

When someone asks, "What time is it?," note that your arm rotated with the palm of the hand rotating down. Try this experiment place your arm above your head and rotate your arm as if someone just asked, "What time is it? " That's pronation. To understand the action of pronation we must understand what part it plays in the serve.

Pronate to Generate Power.

Power—When the racket is behind the back and then snaps to the ball, the action is like a rubber band stretching to its fullest. As the arm accelerates up to the contact point, it is also rotating outward to align the racket face with the ball. The accelerating arm coupled with the rotating arm creates maximum power.

Pronate to Generate Placement

Placement—First we must realize that tennis is a game of opposites; we swing opposite to the direction in which we want the ball to go. That means if we want the ball to move to the left, we must swing the racket towards the right. This generates placement by pronating our arm so it aligns the racket face to the location of the ball, which will result in the ball moving in the intended direction. What is confusing is that the ball goes in the opposite direction of the contact. Too make the ball go wide, you must hit to the outside of the ball.

Pronate to Generate Spin

Spin— To generate spin, pronate by turning the racket face against the backside of the ball and then brushing across the ball, rather than through the ball. This action is similar to peeling an apple.

Serve

Jump Through Hoops!

Many players want to get power on their serve but as they are serving their front leg (closest to the baseline) will actually jump back away from the baseline, pulling their body backwards.

In today's game we are seeing all the touring pros launch and land with their non-dominant leg into the court, which allows the body to move up to strike the ball and then ensures that the player will move into the court, transferring power to the contact point.

To feel this in practice, place a hula hoop in front of you

Then practice serving (without the ball) and jump and land in the hula hoop

After fifteen or twenty times, serve with the ball, still concentrating on launching and landing (not focusing on whether the ball went in or out of the serve court).

Try this and your serve will have your adversary jumping through hoops!

Return of Serve

First Serve, Make Them Play; Second Serve, Make Them Pay

If your opponent was allowed to start each point with an overhead smash you would cry, *No fair!* A serve is just an overhead smash from the baseline. Usually, when returning an overhead, you are trying just to get the ball back in play. Shouldn't that be your objective when your opponent has an aggressive first serve—to get the ball back in play?

The serve is considered the first attacking shot of the point. You must get your racket on the ball even if the return is weak. Many times, even weak returns can bring about a mistake from your opponent. If you have a strong return and can counterattack a strong serve with your return, great! But if you are like me, you are just trying to get your racket on the ball and make your opponent *play*.

The second serve is a different story. Typically, a server is going to be more cautious with a second serve because no player wants to double fault. You should take a more aggressive position by moving forward and attacking that second serve with your return. Make them pay for missing that first serve.

Return of Serve

One, Two, Hop, and Hit

How often do you feel your reaction time just isn't quick enough to return your opponent's blazing serve? Too often, you say? One way to improve a receiver's reaction time lies in the way they set up in the ready position.

The conventional ready position is one in which the receiver is in a low crouch, ready to spring up and at the ball as it comes to them. While this is good for some players, I am a proponent of the receiver starting back a few steps and then timing the move forward with the service motion of their opponent—two steps forward, split-and-hit action.

My reasoning is best illustrated by this example. You are driving a car and you are at a dead stop at a traffic light. As the light turns green, a car pulls along side you. Is your car or the car that just pulled alongside you going to be quicker to move through the intersection? Of course, the car that is still moving is going to be quicker than a car at a standstill. That is the way I see a receiver. By taking two steps back from your normal receiving position and then, as the server starts their service motion, take one step, two steps, split about the same time they are striking the ball. Then hit the ball.

All serves are different—some faster, some slower, some with more spin. The key to returning serve against all players is to adjust your position so you can give yourself the best chance to return serve successfully. Don't always stand in the same place to return all serves.

One, two, hop and hit—you create your own momentum to help you accelerate into the serve.

Return of Serve

Stay Back on Flat, Move In on Spin

After the serve, the return of serve is the second most important stroke in the game, and yet the average returner takes a victim's attitude towards returning: "Yeah right, I can hardly get a racket on that serve much less *aim* my return." Rather than being victimized, learn to turn your return of serve into a weapon like Andre Agassi used to do or Novak Djokovic does today. There are adjustments that returners can make to improve their chances of winning points with an aggressive return.

You need to realize that all servers have their own style of serve—some with more power, some with more spin—and, realize too that the typical receiver will position themselves in the same location for all serves. Be more flexible and adjust to each opponent and *stay back on flat, move in on spin*.

When returning an opponent's flat/hard serve, *stay back* a step or two farther than you normally would to receive. With the average serve arriving in less than a second, these extra steps will give you more time to ready yourself, to read where the ball is being served, and to respond to the ball. The return stroke should be compact—a short backswing with a short follow-through. A receiver wants a quick racket, not a fast racket. What's the difference? A fast racket is accelerating through contact, while a quick racket gets to the contact point quickly.

When faced with a cut or spin serve, you should *move in*. The ball travels at a slower speed with all the energy being stored in the rotation of the ball. Once the ball bounces, the spin then explodes and makes the ball move quickly in the direction of the rotation (spin). A right-hander's slice will move toward your right (server's left), and the left-hander's slice toward your left (server's right). If the right-handed server has a kick serve, then the ball will explode up and toward your left (server's right); and the ball will explode toward your right (server's left) with a left-hander's kick serve. In response to all of the spin serves, you move in to cut the angle of the ball. In other words, you get to the ball before the ball can pull you too far in any direction.

How do you know what serve to prepare for—slice, hard, or kick? Go with the percentages. If 75 percent of the time your opponent has been serving with a spin, then anticipate a spin, and likewise with the flat and kick serves. This means that for three out of four serves, you will be in position to get a good swing at the ball.

"This is great," you say, "but I play against an opponent who can mix up the serve between hard and spin. Now what do I do?" *You act, they'll react.* Just before the server starts into the service motion, move forward or out wide. Let them see you, then move back to your normal position once their eyes go up to watch the toss. This action will cause the server to react to your movement and as we all know, *Winners act, losers react!*

Court Coverage

Hit and Get

Tennis is a game of movement, but unfortunately players have a tendency to hit and watch and wait. Watch to see if the ball is good, wait to see if it's called good, and then wait to see where their opponent hits the ball. Obviously this is too much watching and waiting for a sport designed for constant movement.

To improve court coverage, assume that:

1. the ball you hit is going to be good. You are not out there trying to make mistakes, so why are you waiting for them? On the contrary, you should be surprised when you *do* make a mistake.

2. the ball you hit will come back! You must know that your opponent is trying to make your life miserable during play by getting every shot you hit back to your side of the court. Expect them to get to the ball.

Hit and get ready!

Court Coverage

Feet Move—Swing Smooth

One day, a club member coming off the court responded to my usual "How'd you play?" "Well, I tried a new strategy today, you run to the ball as fast as you can, swing at it as hard as you can and then run to the net as fast as you can and... pick up the ball!"

You say you've tried that strategy too?

Obviously, we don't try to make mistakes on the court, but when we are rushed we *will* make mistakes. What we all need to learn is to move the lower half of our body quickly, particularly the feet, while the upper half, particularly the hands, move smoothly as we approach and hit the ball. This is a little like patting your head while rubbing your stomach—it's tougher than it sounds.

To help execute *feet movement*, say *split* just prior to when your opponent makes contact with the ball. This will reinforce your need to explode in the direction of the ball. As you approach the ball, take little steps to help make any last moment adjustments easier.

Now *swing smooth*. You are now in the right place to hit the ball, and as you start your swing say the word *smoooooth*. By saying smooth slowly, it will make you get your upper body under control as you swing into the ball.

Feet move, swing smooth: a strategy that works!

Court Coverage

Footwork—Adjustment Steps Followed by a Balance Step

Tennis is a game of emergencies. We always seem to be rushing over to a ball or moving and preparing for the next ball. When in motion to strike the ball, we have specific footwork that allows us a more proficient way to not overrun the contact point plus giving us better balance.

1. *Adjustment steps*—These are small, quick steps to the oncoming ball. These small steps allow us to organize our feet prior to contact by making last-moment adjustments.

2. *Balance steps*—This is a longer step. This extended stride (wider than your shoulders) into the contact point of the ball gives you balance on the stroke and more power on the contact.

Court Coverage

Rip and run—When you "rip" a ground stroke and anticipate a weak response from your opponent, run to the net looking for the easy put-away.

Dash and cash—Always look to "cash-in" on your penetrating shots by "dashing" to the net for the ending shot.

Shoot and scoot—Shoot your stroke to the open court and scoot to the follow-up position to win the point.

Rush and crush—You see, or sense, a weak, short-landing ball then rush yourself into the winning position, so you can crush the put-away shot.

Smash and crash—Smash a ground stroke to an area of the court, then crash the net for the put-away.

Court Coverage

Split Step, Not Split Stop

When approaching the net, do not run through the first volley! Most players have been told this numerous times. Some of us have learned it so well that we *stop* as we position ourselves for that volley. This stop will not give you the proper body-weight transfer that you need to generate power on the volley. Moreover, it will diffuse any momentum you had for getting into the next position.

When you are coming to the net, don't think that you have a stop sign in front of you, but rather a yield sign. A yield sign means to slow down, take a quick read of the traffic, and then continue. That is what you want to accomplish with your split step— slow down to ready yourself to change direction, read the direction of the ball, and respond to the ball.

To summarize, when preparing for a first volley, *Ready, read, respond* to yield you more points.

Court Coverage

Split Step—It's When, Not Where

As a teaching pro, I am often asked by students, "Where is the best place on the court to split step when I'm approaching the net?"

It is not *where* on the court you attempt to split step, but *when* you make a split step. You want to time your split step with the moment prior to your opponent's contact with the ball. This timing allows your body to continue its forward momentum, which in turn lets you move more quickly to your opponent's try for a passing shot.

Bear in mind, it's *when,* not *where* you split that generates a better volley.

Court Coverage

Lobs...Don't Have to Be a Four-Letter Word

Running down the lob can be a *very* difficult task, so much so that it keeps players from venturing to the net, not wishing to leave the security of the baseline. However, as tennis instructors we encourage our students to rush the net, and invariably the student responds, "But what about the lob?" Fortunately, there is a way to rushing while also protecting against lobs, and that's what this section will discuss.

1. *Split step*— This was discussed in "Split-Step" above.

2. *Reading*—In tennis we anticipate in three styles, one of which is reading our adversary's body language. When the opponent leans back, it opens the racket face which helps lift the ball. This leaning back signals you to break your forward momentum and ready yourself for the lob.

3. *Drop step*—The mistake many players make is to wait for the ball to get directly over head, or even worse, wait for the ball to bounce before they move. Whether you're hitting an overhead or running it down, you may have waited too long for either to be successful. The correct technique is a "drop-step" back with the dominant side. If you're right-handed, drop step with your right foot.

4. *Beat the ball back there*—Once you decipher where the ball will land, get there before the ball does. Note in the picture how the player is

waiting for the ball to arrive. This will allow you time to set up and decide what your response will be. The earlier you prepare the slower the point seems to play.

5. *Move away from the path of the ball*—When moving for the ball, place the ball to the outside of your dominant shoulder by taking a few steps toward your left, if you are right-handed. Moving in a semicircle will allow you to move away from the flight of the ball and then once it bounces you can move back in toward the ball.

6. *Re-lob*—Once back in position, what do you do? Answer: "re-lob." Since you have turned your back on your opponent, you aren't quite sure where they are on the court—at the net or back at the baseline. This re-lob will afford you time to slow the point down and take a quick scan of the court to see where you are and where your opponent is.

Court Coverage

Absorbing Depth

Tennis is a lower body game. When the lower body (legs) doesn't get you in the correct position, then the upper body has to compensate. The way the upper body compensates is by tilting forward from the waist for the shallow-landing ball or by leaning back from the waist for the deep-landing ball. In this section we offer four tips to cope with the deep-arriving ball.

1. *Drop step back with the right leg*—(for right-handers) This makes your body turn sideways to the net as you move back, inducing the body to prepare the racket, but more importantly keeping the body on-balance as you move back.

2. *Take a firm right foot stance*;—The right leg goes out wider than the shoulders, allowing for a strong foundation and preventing the upper body from leaning back.

3. *Jump up off of the right leg*—This will thrust the body up to create power on the stroke, vertical power.

4. *Left leg stays in front*—The left leg stays in front on the stroke, precluding the upper body from opening the shoulders too early in the swing. Additionally, this will assist in a quicker recovery to the baseline.

Spins and Strokes

Slice—the 3-Ds

Slice (a.k.a. under spin) has made a resurgence in the pro game. I say resurgence because the slice took a backseat to topspin in the eighties and nineties. Now we see touring pros, such as Roger Federer employing a slice backhand tactic, and Kim Clijsters with her famous outstretched wide forehand, or Andy Roddick, with his side-slice backhand approach shot, very effectively used by his former coach Jimmy Connors when he was on the tour.

When deciding to hit a slice you should realize the slice has three varieties: drive, draw, and drop—the 3-Ds. Each of them has a different purpose and all have both similar and diverse behavior. Knowing the similarities, differences, and proper time to hit them is what this section is about.

Drive slice—The racket head starts slightly above the intended contact point, approximately shoulder height, the racket moves down and through the contact of the ball. The arm action resembles the safe sign in baseball. Maintaining the wrist angle is vital, as displayed in the picture below, because it keeps the racket-face angle behind the ball longer, resulting in a lower trajectory and lower bouncing ball.

This tactic is commonly used as an approach shot because a drive slice will take longer to get to the opponent's court giving you more time to get to an advantageous net position. The bounce will stay low, forcing the opponent to hit up over the net, where they run the risk of hitting the ball too high, giving you an easy put-away. Furthermore, if your opponent uses the

Semi-Western or Western grips on their forehand, the drive slice will make their shot particularly difficult to return to you because the Western grip is close the racket face, which does not allow the racket face to get under the ball.

Draw slice—This slice is so named because it is designed to draw (float) up or to draw (bounce) away from the opponent. To draw the ball so it will float, start your racket up above the contact point. Then let the racket face move down, under, and forward. Finally, allow the elbow to drop into the swing followed by a slight wrist drop, as demonstrated.

This swing looks like the letter U. Hit the float when you want more time to get back into proper position, because this shot takes longer to arrive to the opponent's side.

The draw slice that moves, bounces, and moves toward the side of the court away from your opponent is most typically hit as an approach shot. This shot is executed by starting the racket above the ball, just like the other slices, and then pulling your racket across the backside of the ball to create a sideways rotation on the ball. This slice allows you to play with less risk by playing the ball farther away from the sidelines. Once it bounces, it will move away from your opponent and back towards the sidelines, consequently making it more difficult for your opponent to hit an effective passing shot.

The draw slice kills the power given you by the opponent. If your adversary hits the ball harder than you feel confident in returning then use the draw slice to kill their power.

Drop shot—a slice is required for a drop shot for two reasons: 1) a slice will kill the power from the oncoming ball, and 2) once the ball bounces on the opponent's side it will back up or move away from the opponent, making the drop shot more difficult to retrieve. The way you execute the drop shot is by preparing the racket slightly above the intended contact point (the same motion as the drive slice in order to disguise the shot selection). Then, with a relaxed grip on the handle, brush the racket face down and under the backside of the ball.

CURL'S PEARLS

After the drop shot the ball should leave your strings traveling in a low trajectory, or down, but *not* up. If it is traveling up, your opponent will see that it is a drop shot and have time to respond.

The right moment in a point, the proper time in a match, and your positioning on the court are three big considerations for choosing the drop shot. A drop shot should be used as a surprise tactic—when your opponent has little time to see that it's coming. That's why you should only attempt the drop shot from the mid court (no man's land) area. The drop shot can also be used to pressure your opponent by pulling them to the net, where they are uncomfortable.

Two precautionary thoughts regarding the drop shot:

1. Never should a drop shot be used to get you out of trouble. It will only get you into more trouble if used at an inopportune time.

2. If any of these slices are hit with too high a trajectory, greater than 45 degrees, the ball will "sit up" giving the adversary time to step around and hit.

Next slice...Hit it in!

Spins and Strokes

Slice is Nice but Topspin Wins

How does a player influence the ball's movement in the direction they want it to move *after* it leaves their racket? There are two ways that a ball goes into the court: gravity and spin. Let's talk about the two basic spins, slice and topspin.

Slice is nice—The swing on a slice starts above the planned contact point. This creates a high-to-low swing pattern with the strings brushing or glancing down the backside of the ball and a finish swing out in front of the body pointing at the intended target. The ball, when it leaves the racket, will have a rising trajectory; after it hits the court, will move through the court while staying low.

When should you hit slice? It is good to hit slice when you are in a bit of trouble and need additional time to recover. As mentioned, a slice will rise (hopefully not to much) as it goes over the net, which will create some recovery time. It is also good to use slice as an approach shot. A slice approach will give you more time to position yourself at the net. And once the ball bounces, it stays low, forcing your opponent to hit up over the net, which gives you more time to respond to their passing attempt.

Slice is also good to hit on a windy day, especially if a strong wind is in your face. Hit a driving slice, keeping it low, so it will cut through the wind, and let the wind drop the ball in the court.

Now here are the disadvantages of slice. As I said earlier, slice will give you more time to recover; therefore, it will also give your opponent more time to get in position. Be certain you are hitting slice when you want the extra time, *not* when your opponent wants the extra time. Slice can also make the ball rise too much, and cause it to sit up in the opponent's court for an easy put-away. Make sure the ball has a low trajectory to keep it from sitting up.

Topspin wins—Hitting topspin begins with the racket head below the ball and then brushing or glancing up the backside of the ball. The swing finishes up and to the other shoulder. This motion causes the ball to rotate forward and down. The ball will move in the direction of its rotation. Once the ball hits the court, an explosion of speed forces the ball to move forward more quickly. This means that a topspin ball will move down into the court more quickly than a slice. In contrast to the slice, topspin gives the opponent less time to get back into position because of the speed of the spin.

When do you hit topspin? A good occasion is when your opponent is at the net. The reason? You can hit the ball faster and the ball will drop more quickly, making it more difficult for the player to volley the ball. Simply stated, it is harder to volley a ball with a downward movement than it is to volley a ball moving up or traveling straight. Another good time to hit topspin is when a strong wind is at your back. You can use the forward-down rotation of the ball to fight against the wind blowing your shot long.

The downsides of topspin: As I mentioned, the ball gets over the net and down into the court quickly with topspin, but remember, the quicker the ball gets to your opponent, the quicker it can come back to you. Also, sometimes too much topspin may make the ball land shorter than you wanted and invite your opponent forward.

In summary, slice is a more compact swing with control intentions, requiring firmer wrist action; conversely, topspin is a longer, more aggressive stroke with a vertical wrist movement. *Slice is nice, but topspin wins.*

Spins and Strokes

Topspin...Accelerate, Abbreviate, Exaggerate

Today we see the touring pros hitting the ball harder, but still the ball finds the court. You ask, "How do they do that" Can I do it?" They hit the ball harder and still keep it in the court because of topspin. You can own the same control.

A ball moves through the air in the direction of its frontal rotation. When the front of the ball is rotating up, or in reverse, it will have an under-spin movement up, as with a slice. Conversely, when the ball rotates forward with over spin, it will have a movement down known as topspin. That downward movement is what allows the pros to hit the ball harder because the spin directs the ball down onto the court, rather than in a flat trajectory. Topspin also allows a higher net clearance with less chance of netting the shot. When hitting topspin, the arm must complete three jobs for the hit to be successful. If any or all are missing in the stroke, you'll not get the desired result.

1. *Accelerate*—Many times, players hitting topspin will slow their racket before contact which reduces the desired tight rotation of the ball; the ball travels long. You must accelerate the racket *to and through* the contact to impart the desired spin to the ball.

2. *Abbreviate*—There are two topspins—moderate and maximum. A moderate topspin will land the ball deep in the opposing court. To achieve this, lengthen your stroke before finishing with the racket head over the opposite shoulder. To maximize topspin, the stroke is shorter and in a quick, vertical arc with the finish again over the opposite shoulder. This means the more topspin you wish to impart to the ball, the more vertical (abbreviated) your swing should be. Hit it with an exaggerated low-to-high movement that extends the racket face vertically. For moderate topspin, hit low to high but extend the racket forward before completing the finish.

3. *Exaggerate*—Topspin is an exaggerated arm action, as opposed to the slice, which is a shorter arm action, like a punch. The topspin requires a longer arm action, which causes the racket to be traveling faster at moment of impact. The arm action must be looser to throw the racket face behind the ball, which will help exaggerate the required over-the-shoulder finish.

Spins and Strokes

Erase the Space

The opponent many times will hit us balls that have a lot of spin on them, commonly named "junk balls." A ball with much spin moves through the air rather slowly, and we get hypnotized by this slow-moving ball, and we don't move. Then the ball explodes right at our feet when the heavy spin takes control of the ball, and we're caught standing and trying to dig the ball out of our shoelaces.

Erase the space between you and that oncoming ball. Move closer to the ball and get to it before it has time to do much "dancing." Ideally you should take the ball before it bounces, because a spin is most effective once it bounces. Once you get there, hit through the spin. Hitting through the spin will not allow the spin to grab hold of your strings and go into a direction you don't want it to go. In short you *move to it and hit through it.*

The next mistake we make is to take too big a swing at the spinning ball. This large swing doesn't allow for any adjustment to the ball movement. By the time the swing comes to the contact point the ball may have started moving, and we can't adapt our swing to the movement. In more concise terms, *don't swing it, bring it.* That is, don't take a big swing at it, bring the body to it.

Heavy spinning ball? Erase the space between you and the ball.

Spins and Strokes

Less is More

Every time we hit a tennis ball, we energize the ball either by putting energy into the velocity (power) or the rotation (spin) of the ball. Note that when you put spin on the ball, you will take off velocity. Your focus when putting spin on the ball is to train your swing to travel up or down, depending on whether you are hitting slice (down) or topspin (up). In both swings, you want to glance the backside of the ball making *less contact* on the ball but creating *more rotation* on the ball. Next time you desire spin, think: *less will give me more.*

Spins and Strokes

Less is Best

In tennis, the arm is the control source and the body delivers the power, but when hitting volleys players tend to overuse the arm to produce the power. To hit a solid volley, keep in mind that the elbow of your racket arm should be reasonably close to your body at the start of the swing. Move your body to the ball and then shift your body through the contact point.

The next time you volley, let your arm control the racket and let your body give you the power. You'll soon discover, *the less you do the best you'll do.*

Spins and Strokes

If Your Strokes Fail Ya, Hit Australia

Is this a familiar situation? You are stretching wide for a ball. You swing and the ball falls into the net. Your stroke failed you. You're thinking, "I ran all that way to get to the ball just to put it into the net! Why run?"

The next time you are in that situation, *hit Australia.* That's right—Australia! If you look at the tennis ball as if it were the earth, where's Australia? "Down under" the ball.

Next time you're worried that your stroke may fail, take a trip. Make contact at Australia and hear your opponent say, "Good shot, mate."

Spins and Strokes

In Tennis, "But" is the Rule, Not the Exception

The little three-letter word "but" is prominent in the English language and used daily in print and conversation. It is also a frequently applied word in tennis instruction with a second T added to make it "butt." The first association is with the butt of the racket, which plays an essential part in properly completing a forehand or two-handed topspin backhand. The racket butt must finish pointing at the opposing court or you haven't finished the stroke. Illustrations 1 and 2 show the butt at completion.

The racket has imparted maximum topspin and power with this finishing vertical wrist action. All the topspin players (most of the touring pros) complete the stroke with a snap of the racket around the opposite shoulder. That movement is ensured when the racket butt points to the target area.

CURL'S PEARLS

Another important role of the racket butt is in volleying. Keep the butt of the racket lower than the racket head on all volleys, especially on the low returns when the tendency to drop the head is the greatest.

When the racket head drops below the wrist in net play, power is lost, resulting in a netted ball or a pop-up sitter for the opponent. This is logical when you think about it as hand wrestling. You are much stronger with your hand up (when the racket butt would point downward) than if you reversed your hand, which would point the butt above your hand.

A powerful hand position.

A weakened hand position

If there is a more difficult tennis shot, it's the low shot. We are told, and we tell ourselves, to bend the knees, but too often we take a short cut to the ball by bending at the waist.

Demonstrates the wrong body position when handling low balls, racket head drops and butt goes out.

There goes your butt in the opposite direction of the shot flight and with it goes your power and just about everything else necessary for a good return. Get your butt down! Extend the front foot toward the oncoming ball with the knee bent and at the same time drop your butt, forcing the trailing knee to bend even lower. This action keeps the upper body perpendicular and behind the shot, and directs the racket to contact the ball with the face perpendicular. From a balanced, lower center of gravity there is longer hitting zone making for a more consistent shot.

Note that the back knee is lower in the stance to assure proper balance and weight transfer.

When striking the ball you have many placement options. Ask, "Do I hit in front of my opponent or hit behind them." Hit in the direction your opponent's *butt* is pointing. When you have them running to recover, hit behind them.

Player going in the wrong direction, away from the ball.

This is often called "wrong footing." It requires the opponent to reverse direction, recover their balance, and then make the return—all to your advantage—when you hit where their butt is pointed.

One more desirable butt action is in the serve. Your power will mostly originate from the rotation and then uncoiling of your body into the serve. Tennis is a lower body sport. When the lower body doesn't perform correctly, there has to be upper body compensation. Therefore if you don't rotate your butt (lower body) you won't make the upper body rotation necessary for the best serve.

Lower body in coiling, therefore, the upper body does not have to work as hard.

Right-handers should think, "rotate the left butt cheek," and lefties, "the right butt cheek." This will corkscrew your body from the butt through the shoulders for maximum power into the ball at the point of contact.

Following these simple "butt" points could mean you will no longer be the butt of your club jokes and you might even butt heads successfully with your club champ.

Spins and Strokes

The K.I.S. Swing—Keep It Simple

As teaching professionals, from time to time we tend to complicate something as simple as the swing. An uncomplicated but precise way of looking at the swing is to focus on the two actions that are part of all swings, the take back and the forward swing. These two actions are the responsibility of the upper and lower body. In the details described below, I am referring to the forehand, but this body action translates to the backhand side as well.

The upper body starts the swing back—The upper body starts the racket back with a rotating (turning) of the shoulders and hips, known as the "unit turn". Note how the body is coiled properly, the shoulders rotating more than the hips, with the non-dominant arm placed across—in front of—the body. These actions help load the body onto the back leg, allowing for the proper uncoiling into the stroke. If the racket arm takes the racket back *independently* of the non-dominant side, then the dominant side must work twice as hard to create the desired power because the upper body is no longer working as a unit.

The lower body initiates the swing forward—The back knee (right knee for right-handers, left knee for left-handers), is the impetus that advances the swing forward by rotating inward in a counterclockwise movement (clockwise for the left hander). This triggers the release of the upper body, starting with the hips, followed by the trunk, then the shoulders, and finally the arm. This unit-turn action is what makes the stroke so effortless. To get the feel of this unit turn, take a five- or ten-pound medicine ball and shift it from one side of the body to the other. Note how the lower body is rolling with the legs turning inward.

To summarize, upper body starts it back, lower body starts it forward. Incorporate this and *KISS* your stroke problems good-bye.

Spins and Strokes

Feel or Touch

You're watching a tennis match on TV and the announcer declares, "Roger Federer has great touch around the net," or "Roger Federer has great feel for his volleys." What does the announcer mean by those statements, and how can you, the tennis-playing observer, incorporate it into your game?

Feel or touch, as this author defines it, is the pressure (or lack of pressure) one places on the handle (grip) prior to and just after contact of the ball. An experiment I encourage you to try is to place a racket on the ground as you see in picture below;

then step on the handle and drop a ball from shoulder height, note the rebound elevation.

This stepping on the handle represents a squeezing pressure on the handle at the moment of contact that you, the player, place on the racket. This squeezing makes the ball go back deeper in the court.

A *squeeze and freeze* is a squeezing of the handle just at the moment of impact. This squeezing of the handle reduces the give of the racket, making the racket play more stiffly, with the energy of the oncoming ball being used to send it back deep and crisply. The freeze just after contact is made ensures a short, compact volley motion.

A *relax and bounce back* is the next way we can feel or touch the ball. Using the previous example, drop a ball from shoulder height *without* the foot being on the handle.

Notice that the ball's rebound is much lower than in the previous experiment. This represents a relaxed grip on the handle. This relaxed grip will allow the wrist to absorb all the force of impact and the racket will bounce opposite (back) from the direction that the ball is moving. Consequentially, the ball will land short; the result is a drop volley or an angle volley.

There are different degrees of firmness that you apply to your handle, giving you the depth—short or deep—that you desire on the shot. This is something that only experience and experimentation can teach you. To help you learn about feel, have someone hit a ball to you; try to catch it on your strings. It teaches you to allow the racket to soften up at contact, a feel that you need for your shots.

Spins and Strokes

I Have to Hand it to You—Quick Hands, Fast Hands, Soft Hands

The tennis announcer (or coach) talks about quick hands with hurried shots, or says that the baseline player has fast hands when making ground strokes, or soft hands around the net. What's this all about? Can it be added to the club player's game? It's easily understood and can be learned with a few basics. First, though, you must understand that quick hands and fast hands are two different things and are accomplishing different results.

1. *Quick hands*—This describes the hand movement from the ready position to the contact point. Quick hands are needed for the balls coming at you swiftly. The racket must be ready. Do this by getting from the ready position to the contact point by taking the shortest route. The stroke really isn't a stroke; it has no backswing or follow-through. We typically need quick hands for reaction shots such as volleys, return of serve, and deep-landing ground strokes. All are in response to a well-hit shot, using the force of the incoming shot to send the ball back.

2. *Fast hands*—This is when the racket travels farthest before reaching the contact point, which creates power in the shot. To create a fast racket (hands), the normal backswing is made with the racket building up speed prior to and through contact with the ball. Fast hands are generally used in aggressive forehand ground strokes, overheads, swinging volley, and some approach shots, and primarily on the serve. The serve is the longest stroke in tennis—longest in length and the time it takes to execute. And since the serve is the longest stroke, that is also why for many it is the most difficult stroke to learn. It has farther to travel, which often influences the stroke adversely. All of the fast-hands strokes are executed to be *point-ending* or *taking-control* shots.

3. *Soft hands*—This is softening of the hands for the required control and the desired depth on your shot. The adversary will hit hot,

(a fast-traveling ball), and you desire to take all the power off their shot. This is executed by absorbing the contact into the racket hand, relaxing the grip on the racket just at the moment of impact; a relaxed grip deadens the hit. You need soft hands for drop shots, drop volleys, angles, lobs, and shots you want to place at the net rusher's feet.

In summary, we *create power* with fast hands, we *use power* with quick hands, and we *kill power* with soft hands.

Spins and Strokes

Framing Contact

When a reporter asked Babe Ruth, "What's your secret to hitting?" Ruth replied, "I let the pitcher pitch and when the ball gets right there"—pointing his finger at a spot in front of him—"that's when I hit it."

Ruth was referring to the contact point, and whether it is baseball, golf, or tennis, the contact point is *everything*. It doesn't matter if you're receiving a slice, topspin, high bounce or low, what matters is that when it gets to your contact point you hit the ball.

Establishing your contact point on strokes does several things:

1. It doesn't allow for any negative thoughts. Your thoughts are focused on what you are planning to carry out, not what happened in the past or worse yet, worrying about the consequence if you should lose the point. In short, you are staying *in the now*.

2. It doesn't allow us to observe where the adversary is. Once again we are focused on ourselves and not the opponent. Where they are and what

they are anticipating makes no difference. All that matters is you and your contact of the ball.

How to establish your contact point: Place your racket on your forehand side at the point where the arm is most relaxed. Now do the same on the backhand side, all the while looking at the racket position. Those racket placements are *your* contact points for those strokes, where you are most comfortable striking the ball. You should attempt to hit the ball from there all the time.

Let's go back to Babe Ruth's words: "I let the pitcher pitch it and when the ball gets right here…that's when I hit it." He is framing contact. He places an imaginary frame (window) around the area where he is most comfortable striking the ball, and when the ball comes into that frame (window), he strikes it. Place a frame around the contact point, watch the ball come into that frame, and when it gets there, hit a home run!

Anticipation

Know What Area You're In, Know What Shot to Select,

Know What Area Your Opponent is In, Know What Shot to Expect

When you're playing basketball and you have the ball, are you playing offense or defense? Answer: offense. When you're playing soccer and the opposing team has the ball, are you playing offense or defense? Answer: defense. When you're playing tennis and you're hitting the ball, are you playing offense or defense? Answer: depends. That's what makes tennis unique compared to many other sports. When you are hitting the ball, you may be playing either offense or defense.

First we must understand that a player hits each ball with one of three intentions: to be offensive, defensive, or neutral. Your position on the court can guide you as to what shot to select. There are four zones to a tennis court as shown in the court diagram: defensive, rally, attack, and offensive. You should learn the location of each zone, the shots you should select in each, and what your next position should be after you complete your stroke.

The defensive zone is located two feet behind the baseline and all the way back to the fence. When you hit the ball from the defensive zone, you should be intent on hitting a defensive shot such as a lob or a looper. After a defensive shot, you should recover to the rally position on the court in most situations. I say in *most* situations because you may find that you have hit such a great lob that it drives your adversary all the way back to their fence. If that happens, you can anticipate a weak return and, by moving forward a few steps into the court, pounce on their weak response.

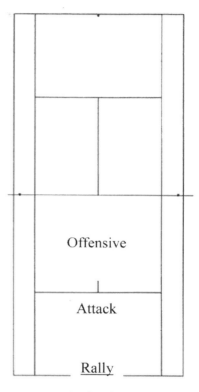

The rally zone is approximately two feet in front of the baseline to two feet behind the baseline. Your objective is to aim your strokes three to five feet above the net. (Refer to *Three to Five to Stay Alive* later in this chapter.) In the rally zone, your strokes are more neutral. You use your basic forehand and backhand strokes that you learned as a beginner. You may not always win points with your rally strokes, but you certainly do not want to lose any. After you hit a rally-zone shot you will most likely stay in the rally zone. A related fact: most points are lost in the rally zone because players are attempting to hit a shot that is more offensive shot than they need.

The attack zone is located approximately two feet in front of the baseline (at the front of the rally zone) to two feet behind the service line. Your thinking should be more aggressive there than it is when you are in the defensive and rally zones. Your focus is on hitting the ball to your opponent's weaknesses, hitting the ball with power, or making your opponent run. To attack, you must hit the ball when it is high in your hitting zone, waist level to shoulder height. Hitting the ball at this height eliminates any concern about the net and allows you to hit through the ball to create more power. The strokes you will most often find yourself using in the attack zone will be, among others, the slice-approach shots, the "killer" forehands (such as Andre Agassi's notorious forehand from mid court), drop shots, and the mid-court volleys. All of these strokes are intended to do damage to your opponent. You should expect a weak response from any of those shots, so your next position should be at the net—the offensive zone.

The offensive zone is located at the front of the attack zone (two feet behind the service line) and all the way to the net. Your thinking in this zone is to end the point, whether it is by your winning shot or by your opponent's losing shot. You should be aggressive with your strokes but not so aggressive that you miss an easy put-away. You most likely will hit overhead smashes and volleys, both of which are considered offensive strokes. If you have executed these strokes correctly, your next position is in the winner's circle.

To summarize: Try to be cognizant of which zone you are hitting from—the defensive, the rally, the attack, or the offensive, and make your shot selections match your zone. Learn to anticipate what shot your opponents will select by recognizing what area of the court they are in when they hit the ball. If they are in the attack zone, then you can expect an attacking shot, and so forth. One word of caution: the only absolute in tennis is that there are no absolutes; expect exceptions to the rules above.

Anticipation

Approach Shots—You Get or You Give

An approach shot is one that you hit and then approach the net. Recognizing opportunities to attack your opponent is one of the first ingredients in applying pressure to your adversary. First, you must know the attacking game.

To know the attacking game, (a.k.a. the approach shot), you must understand that the approach shot is the third most important stroke in the game of tennis. Why? Because if you hit a good approach, *you have control of the point*, but if you hit a bad approach, then *your opponent has control of the point*.

Next, you must realize that there are two types of approach shots: the type you get and the type you give. The approach that you get is the most typical approach shot. You are at the baseline, rallying, and you get a short-landing ball from your opponent. You move forward into the attack zone and hit it and then move farther forward to take an aggressive position at the net.

The second type of an approach shot is the kind you give. You are rallying with your opponent and in that rally you notice that you hit such a strong shot that your opponent is stretching to get to the ball (see *When They're Stretching…You're Fetching*). You can anticipate a weak response, so you should go forward to the net to knock off the anticipated "sitter." Another approach opportunity is when you are in a rally and you throw up a deep lob. You notice your opponent is backing up to allow the ball to bounce. Again, you should move forward to anticipate a "floater" ball coming back. In both of these situations—and in a few more—you have given yourself the approach shot opportunity.

Unbelievably, the given approach shots usually go unclaimed by most tennis players. Next time, be sure to capitalize on getting or giving when it comes to the attacking game.

Anticipation

When They're Stretching, You're Fetching

Opportunities to attack an opponent come and go so quickly that most of the time they go undetected. Below are two keys to help you see and seize those attack openings by reading your opponent's body language:

1. When your adversary is moving away from the baseline or when their body is off balance as they stroke the ball, you should use both of those moments to move forward in anticipation of a weak or shallow-landing ball.

2. When you have your opponent on the full stretch, usually when they are pulled out wide of the court, get ready to fetch a feeble or short-landing ball.

Remember, if they are moving away or if they are *stretching*...you should be *fetching*!

Anticipation

See Their Buns, You Run

Tennis and boxing are very similar. In both sports, participants are trying to deliver the knockout blow, and like a boxer, a tennis player has to be able to see and seize the opportunity to hit the knockout blow. Also, in both sports, by reading the opponent's body language you can tell if and when you have them in trouble. And if you don't know you have your adversary in trouble, then you are letting a good opportunity slip away.

In tennis, one see-and-seize opportunity is when your opponent is running away from the net to make a shot on a ball that you hit. You should expect a weak response shot because they are moving away from the court and it will be difficult for them to get much power on their stroke. As they are moving back to retrieve your shot and when you see their *buns*, that is your signal to *run* forward to give the knock-out blow.

Anticipation

If They Don't Show It, Then You Don't Know It

It's 4–all in the third set and you are thinking, *Are they going to serve and volley or serve to my backhand?* Or when playing doubles you might wonder, *Are they going to hit down my alley?* Sound like the conversations going on in your head? My question to you is, has any one tried any of those tactics before in the match? If they haven't then it is probably because they don't own those shots. You should clear your mind of any thoughts that anticipate tactics and only worry about the tactics that your opponent has *successfully shown*.

I was watching a doubles team that I coached. They would run to the net as a team and then the opponents would throw up a lob that went long. This same scenario happened five times, and all five times the lob went long. I noticed that my team kept coming to the net but stayed farther away from the net. The lobs stopped but the passing shots from the opponents were landing at my team's feet, which was working for the opponents.

After my team lost I asked, "Why did you all stop closing into the net?"

The answer—which I must admit I knew was coming— was, "Every time we came into the net they lobbed us, so we thought we'd stay farther back to get to them."

I responded, "I counted all the lobs. You all came to the net five times early in the match, and all five times they lobbed it long, so your attitude toward your opponents should be 'please try more, you obviously don't own that shot!'"

Before you change a tactic, make sure that what your opponent is trying is working to their advantage. If they are trying something that is working to *your advantage*, don't change anything.

As the title reads, *if they don't show it, then you don't know it*. In other words, if they show it and it isn't working, let them hit more.

Anticipation

What You See is What You Get

This saying was made popular by a well-known comedian; here I'll be using it in the context of tennis. I trust it will give you a unique way to recognize when to attempt a winning shot and how to identify where to place that shot.

Stand at the baseline. What part of the court do you see on the opposite side of the net? None! Now start moving forward. What part of the court do you see above the net from the service line? The back part of the court. Move forward again and stop halfway between the service line and the net. What do you see above the net? You can see most of the other side, and as you keep moving forward, you will be able to see much more court.

TENNIS: PLAY SMARTER NOT HARDER II

The court that you see above the net represents a high percentage of shot selections. Notice also that as you move closer to the net, more court opens up to you, thereby giving you more options for winning a point. So the court that you see above the net is where you get to put the ball away for a winner. Conversely, if you see no court then you should attempt no winners.

Therefore, *what you see is what you get.*

Tactics

Hitting the Right Shot to the Right Spot

Tennis can be divided up into two segments: what stroke to use to hit the ball and where to hit the ball. If you have one segment but not the other, you only have a 50 percent chance of winning the point. Let's take a closer look at these two areas.

1. *Hitting the right shot*—When a ball is coming to your side of the court, you have to make a split-second decision. What is the best stroke (shot) to send this ball back into your opponents side? As you consider the answer, keep in mind both your opponent's court location and your own. You must do all of this is to achieve the desired result—winning the point.

Here's an example of a bad shot decision: You are back at the baseline. Your opponent is standing so close to the net they could touch the net with their hand. Your chosen shot is a...drop shot. *Wrong!* You may have hit the best drop shot of your life (good shot), but your opponent is standing right where you are going to hit the ball (wrong spot).

In this scenario, the right shot to the right spot is a lob over the backhand side. A lob because your opponent is standing too close to the net, leaving much of the court behind them open, and over the backhand side of your opponent for the "insurance." By lobbing high over the backhand, you are sending the ball into the most powerless stroke area in the game of tennis. If your lob is low but still on the backhand side, you are still insuring that your opponent will *not* hit an aggressive shot off the lob. A lob over the backhand side will buy the insurance you need to protect yourself from unfortunate happenings. On the other hand, if your lob goes low to the forehand side, you have no insurance against a powerful overhead.

2. *Hitting to the right spot*—You must direct the ball to an area of the court that gives your opponent the most difficulty in returning the ball. Most of the time, you would want to hit the ball to the open court or to your opponent's weakness. (See Chapter II, "Diagnosing Weaknesses.") If your opponent is serving and volleying, one of your options is be to hit the ball to the spot at the "T" (where the service line and center line meet). That will drop the ball at the server's feet forcing them to hit their first volley up over the net, reverse the flight of the ball, and bring it back down into the court. This up-and-down requirement makes it very difficult for your opponent to hit a winning first volley. The tactic is *the right shot to the right spot*.

Tactics

Three to Five to Stay Alive

Every ball we hit falls into one of three categories: offense, defense, and neutral. It is in the neutral category where far too many mistakes are made. When you hit the neutral shot, you should aim three feet above the net. This will give the ball a longer air life and give you more time to recover to an ideal court position. More important, it will give you the added assurance that it will clear the net.

CURL'S PEARLS

In addition to the three feet above the net, aim five feet from the baseline or sidelines. By keeping the ball this close to the baseline, it will prevent your opponents from moving forward into an attacking (offensive) position. By directing your shot five feet from the sideline, the ball will maneuver your opponents sideways or off the court and prevent them from mounting any offense.

Next time when you are in neutral, *three to five to stay alive* in the point.

Tactics

Passing Shot Patterns—Dip and Rip

When being pressured by an opponent positioned at the net, the tendency is to try to hit the ball right through them, hitting the ball too forcefully. With this tactic you may have a few successful passing shots, but usually you have many more unforced errors.

To get past a net person, you need to create an opening for the passing attempt and then execute the passing shot (a passing shot pattern). One way to create an opening is to *dip* your first shot, with topspin, at the feet of the approaching player. This will force the net person to volley the ball up over the net and leave them in a defensive net position, as you move in to *rip* the passing shot by them.

Tactics

Passing Shots Patterns—Dump and Jump

Another way to open the court up for your passing lanes is to dump and jump. In this setting, dump refers to hitting a chip (slice) down at the net rusher's feet, dumping the ball low with little or no power. (The application of slice is discussed in this chapter under *Slice—the 3 Ds*.) This low ball, hit with very little power, will force the net rusher to create all the power and thus risk being too aggressive. Usually, the net rusher will respond with a short volley that will bounce up and make it easier for you to jump on their weak shot and make your pass comfortable.

Tactics

Passing Shot Patterns—High and Low

Another pattern is hitting a lob over the established net player; this will slow them down from rushing in so quickly. After their hit, you have opened up the area in front of your opponent, giving you the low passing path.

Rather than trying to slam passing shots through your opponent, these passing patterns—dip and rip, dump and jump, and high…low—are designed to help you prevent panic when your opponent is either at the net or coming to the net.

Tactics

Rules that Apply to Any Sport

1. *If it ain't broke; don't fix it.* Never change a winning game. If you are like me, you probably over-analyze your match in progress and end up abandoning your game plan by trying different strokes that are just not yours. Don't misunderstand me; it is important to develop your game by adding new shots, but you should try them in a practice setting, not a match setting. During a match, stick with what is working for you.

2. *Dance with who brung ya!* The best way to play a match is *your* way to play a match. Nobody knows your game and its strengths better than you, so stay with your game. If your style has gotten you as far as it has in tennis, why change?

3. *If you're losin', start cruisin'.* Always change a losing game plan. Here's an analogy. You're driving your car, and you get a flat tire. What would you do? (One client I posed this question to said, "I'd call AAA!") Of course the answer is, change the flat tire. It's the same in tennis. Don't wait until the match is over to realize that you should have changed your game. Ideally you should have a plan B when you walk onto the court. When to change? If you lost the first set 6–0, 6–1, or 6–2, you need to change your game plan. What to change? A detailed discussion about changing your game style is included in Chapter II "Diagnosing Weaknesses."

Tactics

Take the Ball on the Rise and Give Them a Surprise

There are two times when the ball is on the rise: when it is rising up over the net and coming towards you, and as it is rising up off the court after it bounces. I am referring to the rise of the ball after it bounces.

The advantages of hitting on the rise are two:

1. It changes the pace to a quicker tempo that may hurry and surprise your opponent into a mistake, and

2. It gives your opponent less recovery time.

To take the ball early requires some adjustments in your stroke. First, a shorter backswing is essential. This allows for better timing on the stroke. Second, you need good balance. To hit on the rise, you must arrive early to the contact point. A precautionary word: hit the ball on the rise because you *want* to not because you *have* to. That being said, when should you take the ball on the rise? When you want to regulate the pace. In this situation, getting the ball back quicker can throw off the rhythm of your opponent's strokes, which may cause more miss-hits on their part. Another good time is when you have your opponent out of position and want to allow as brief a recovery time as possible. This is similar to a fast break in basketball. It doesn't allow the opposing team time to recover and defend, which is the same effect that hitting a ball on the rise has on your opponent. Just remember that when trying to hurry your opponent, you could end up hurrying yourself and creating your own mistakes.

Take the ball on the rise with a shorter backswing and good balance and surprise your unsuspecting opponent.

Tactic

Don't Retreat, Take the Heat

When a deep-landing ball comes to you, you have two options. You can back up and give yourself more time, or you can hold your ground and not back up. When backing up you must realize that you are giving yourself more time, but you are also giving your opponent more time. You weigh the risks and rewards and decide what to do.

There are two situations in which you don't want to back up. First, when your opponent is coming into the net or at the net. By backing up you are giving your opponent more time to get into an advantageous net position plus—and what's more important—since you have moved back, your passing shot will take longer to get to the target. This gives the adversary more time to read where your target is and respond to your shot. Second, you don't wish to back up when your opponent is in a poor court position and they want time to recover. By not retreating, you don't afford them the time.

So *don't retreat...take the heat.*

Doubles Teamwork

Down the Middle Solves the Riddle

When playing doubles, you will often find yourself facing the situation you see in the picture. Because your opponents are positioned at the net, you are forced to hit a passing shot. You are asking yourself, "Where do I hit my passing shot?" When you're hitting a passing shot in doubles, and you do not have a clear shot selection, then you must choose between four passing windows: down the line, down the middle, cross-court angle, or lob. The answer to your query is...down the middle. Why?

Hitting down the middle of your opposition offers three advantages. First, you are usually hitting the ball over the lowest part of the net. Second, you are giving your opponents absolutely no angle, so it will be difficult for them to return with angle (refer to "You Get What You Give" in the Curlyisms chapter). Third, hitting between your opponents will frequently cause confusion among them, with either both or neither trying for the ball.

This brings me back to the riddle: Where do you hit the ball? The old saying has it right. *Down the middle solves the riddle!*

Doubles Teamwork

Sliding and Deciding

Have you ever been at the net with your partner when the lob goes up and in unison you yell, "Yours!" There is a way to keep this from happening. As partners, you both should be *sliding* back to the ball, and then the player who is being lobbed over should be *deciding* who should hit it. The person being lobbed over is the air traffic controller. They know better than you on some basic issues: if they can get to the ball, what stroke they need to hit it with, and how confident they are with that stroke. Your job is to keep your partner informed if you think the ball is going out or what moves your opponents are making.

Sliding and deciding will eliminate the problem of partners going behind each other to be there just in case, or each player calling the other one off the ball.

Doubles Teamwork

Poaching – Fake It Till You Make It

There are two adages that apply to all sports: never change a winning game plan, and always keep your opponent off balance. In tennis, one way to keep your opponent off balance is to poach. Half of the art of poaching is to conceal the fact that you are poaching. To learn that art, practice fake poaching.

In doubles, the usual time to poach or fake poach is when your partner is serving. The receiver has to watch the ball, watch what position the server takes after serving, and watch to see if you are poaching. That's three things to watch with only two eyes.

When should you poach? When your opponents least expect it. It could be the first point of the match. This tactic will catch them by surprise and confuse them for the rest of the match. Even if it is not a success, it will plant a seed in the opponents' minds. And because it is the first point, it has no bearing on the outcome of the rest of the match. Another good time to poach is following an unsuccessful poach; your opponent expects you to "stay at home" because you failed on the last attempt.

Successful poaching relies on timing as well. If you move too soon, your opponent can adjust as necessary to "burn" you. One clue that your opponent has committed to their shot is when their eyes go down to look at the contact point. *Move too soon, you'll look like a baboon!*

When to fake? Anytime you are not really poaching. In other words, you should not be standing still at the net. A good time to fake is right after a successful poach. Your opponents want to embarrass you because you embarrassed them with your poach, so set this play up with your serving partner: your partner serves out wide, and you fake. The receiver, watching you to keep from being burned again, will probably hit the ball down your alley and right to where you are waiting. Timing on the fake is most important. You must fake poach early enough for your opponent to make the adjustment in their swing and hit it right to you. *Fake too late, they won't take the bait!*

Finally, what is the secret to being a successful poacher? It's not timing, it's not technique, it's not when. The most important tip I can give you to be a successful poacher is have a very forgiving partner. We will all attempt to poach and will all be unsuccessful at times. When our partner does attempt a poach, be supportive whether they are successful or not. Remember, the purpose behind a poach or a fake is to keep your opponent off balance.

Doubles Teamwork

Poaching – Disguise to Neutralize

Much of your success in poaching will lie in your ability to disguise when you are doing it. Keeping the adversary off-balance will neutralize the effectiveness of your rivals' shots. Anytime you poach during doubles it acts as a neutralizer, forcing the adversaries to think twice before they execute a shot that you poached on earlier in the competition. As tennis players, we all know that when we're undecided about where to place the ball, the outcome is usually not favorable for us.

Doubles Teamwork

Poaching – Hit the Way You Move, Then Move the Way You Hit

When poaching in doubles, a common mistake is for the poacher to hit the ball behind them (in the opposite direction in which they are moving), as illustrated by the "No" arrow. This shot selection places the poaching team in a vulnerable position by leaving half of the court open for the opponent's winning shot represented by the "Box".

The correct shot for the poacher is to hit the ball in the direction the poacher is moving. This keeps the ball in front of them and leaves them in a better position for their opponent's response the "Yes" arrow. After the poacher hits the ball in the direction in which they are moving, their weight momentum will move them in the correct direction.

Doubles Teamwork

Position without Possession

Let's use a basketball team as an example. There are five players on the floor and one has possession of the ball. The other four teammates are constantly moving for position to take a pass, rebound, score, or get into defensive positions.

Doubles is a team sport, in which one member of the team is serving, returning a shot, etc. The one hitting the ball dictates the play, but the partner must react to support the success of the shot or serve. As in basketball, the non-hitter's movement can make the difference between scoring or losing the point. This means the player not striking the ball must move instinctively with the partner to capitalize on the opportunity created by the hitting partner and together closing the court to an attempt to penetrate your defense. Movement and position when not hitting the ball as well as when hitting is essential.

Stand around when your partner is controlling the play and you'll soon be without partners.

Doubles Teamwork

Hug and Hover

When playing doubles there are three basic formations;

1. Both partners at the net

2. Both partners at the baseline

3. One up, one back

In this article I would like to discuss the formation, both partners at the net. This formation is taught the most by the teaching pros and played the most by the touring pros. The reason is that more than half of the points are won at the net in doubles.

Club players like the one-up–one-back formation because of its simplicity. We often hear, "I'll take the front and you take the back". The problem with this formation is you have one partner playing offensive tennis (the net player) and one partner playing defensive tennis (the baseline player), but they are on the same team. Both have the same goal—winning the point—but each is going about it differently, which doesn't fit the team-sport concept of doubles.

To clear up the confusion when both are at the net, let's talk about *hug and hover*. To understand hug and hover, we must first examine the four passing lanes of your opponents:

1. down the alley

2. down the middle

3. cross-court angle

4. lob

You can see in the diagram that when the ball is hit to the left, the team moves left; conversely when the ball is hit to the right, the team moves right. In doing this, one player moves toward the line and back a few steps. This person's job is to *hover* near the line to cover the alley attempts and back to protect against the lob. Their partner *hugs* the net so they can play balls directed down the middle and they move close to the net to shrink the opponents' angle area.

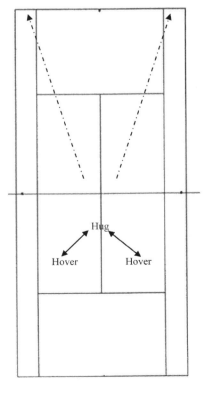

Warning: when both players are at the net, you are forcing your opponent to hit winners, and they *will* hit winners. Say "good shot" and get on with the next point.

In conclusion, to stop wondering whose ball it is when you're at the net with your partner, the hug and hover is the answer to your questions.

CHAPTER 2

Diagnosing Weaknesses

I never lost...I just didn't find my opponent's weakness in time.

—Jimmy Connors

Try solving this puzzle:

You have three rings. One ring can withstand thirty pounds of pressure; the second ring can withstand twenty pounds of pressure; and the third ring can withstand ten pounds. You link the three rings together. How much pressure can these rings withstand? Sixty pounds? More? Less? Need a hint? A chain is only as strong as its weakest link, and according to tennis great Pancho Gonzales, "A tennis player is only as good as their weakness."

Every tennis player has a weakness. You must find that weakness. Once you have found it, focus your attention on it. However, finding that weakness isn't always easy. My coach would often tell me, "Hit it to their backhand," but it's not so simple. In this chapter we will examine the strengths and weaknesses of various strokes, grips, and playing styles. As you absorb this information, keep in mind that *there is no right or wrong way to hit a tennis ball, just effective and ineffective ways.*

The first rule is to always play your game or style of tennis using your strengths. The key is to make your opponent react to you. Establishing your game early will help you avoid wasting time searching for your opponent's weakness.

Grips...Know Their Soft Spots

Every Grip Has a Strength...and a Weakness

One key to a player's ability to reach a higher level of play is to have versatility with his or her grip. A player must be able to utilize the strength of each grip while avoiding its weakness. Being versatile allows you to quickly adjust when encountering different court surfaces, playing styles, ball placement, spins, and height of contact. Versatility will raise the level of your game and leave no soft spots with your grip.

The three basic grips are the Eastern, the Continental, and the Western. First, let's examine the weakness of the grip that is taught most by teaching pros.

The Eastern Forehand Grip—The Eastern Forehand, also known as the "shake-hands" grip, is the most comfortable grip for the novice player to use. This grip is so adaptable that any player can vary their style of play. It can generate good power and depth. The slice is the more comfortable spin, but topspin can be hit with a fair amount of ease. While the Eastern Forehand is comfortable and easy, the Eastern Backhand grip can be difficult to master in the beginning because of the additional time needed to develop the arm and upper body strength necessary to hit this stroke well.

Areas of Weakness:

1. Balls that bounce high (chest height or higher) and low-bouncing balls (knee height or lower) give this grip trouble, because the Eastern grip

has limited wrist movement. Wrist movement enables a player to create excessive spin on the ball, and spin is how a tennis player confronts varying heights.

2. Net play can be troublesome with this grip due to the short reaction time you have at the net. A typical ball will get from the opponent's racket to the net person in less than a second. Not much time to read, react, and change grips. Players who use the Eastern grip at the net will have trouble with low volleys because the hand is positioned behind the racket handle in such a way that it does not open the racket face. The open racket face is needed to ensure that the ball clears the net.

3. As mentioned before, the player with an Eastern grip will have some topspin and some slice, but not an excessive amount. Without excessive spins, the player can not hit the short topspin angles known as "buggy whips" or have too much success with topspin lobs.

Question: How do you play against a player using the Eastern grip?

Answer: You hit with extreme topspin and slice to keep the ball very high (topspin) or very low (slice) in the hitting zone. This excessive spin will help keep your opponent's timing off, causing them to miss-hit more often. However, the Eastern grip player will have penetrating power that send the ball behind your hitting zone quickly. In response to this tactic, you should take a shorter backswing for early preparation and hit low and short to the forehand side. Remember that players who use the Eastern Forehand have trouble with volleying because they need to change grips. Bring them in with short, low-bouncing balls. Throughout his tennis career, Jimmy Connors was plagued with low, short forehand difficulties because he uses the Eastern Forehand grip. You may want to keep this in mind the next time you play Jimbo.

The Western Grip—Players who use this grip are normally power hitters who play a baseline game. They particularly like clay court surfaces and are very effective at putting topspin on the ball. Often these players will have two-fisted backhands. Many of today's touring pros use the Semi-Western or Western grip.

Areas of Weakness:

1. Topspin is the only comfortable spin used with this grip. You can almost eliminate the use of strokes such as a slice approach and drop shot, unless they are capable to change their grip.

2. Other areas of difficulty for the Western and Semi-Western grip users include balls that bounce lower than the knees and balls that are hit late in the stroking stance. In both situations, the racket face is closed and the player will often net many of the balls.

3. The Western grip should not be used at the net for two reasons. First, this grip does not handle low balls very well because, as noted above, the racket face is positioned in a downward slant and can not give the ball the required lift. Second, when hitting a volley, you want under spin on the ball to assure that the ball stays low after the bounce making it more difficult for your opponent to pass you. The western grip does not place under spin on the ball effectively.

Question: How do you play against a Western grip?

Answer: Use a slice to keep the ball low and to kill their power. If your opponent uses a Western grip when they approach, take note of this during warm up. This is a sure sign that they will have trouble with low volleys and backhand volleys. Bring them in if they don't change grips at the net. Their topspin will lack depth on many of their shots, be ready to attack when given the opportunity. Slice serve wide to either side to make them stretch. When stretching the western grips aren't able to apply

DIAGNOSING WEAKNESSES

much topspin to the ball. Be prepared for long rallies; the player with a Western grip has trouble changing direction in their shots, particularly if playing on clay.

The Continental Grip—This grip favors the slice spin, which gives a player good control and consistency. This grip is best for low and stretching balls because it opens the racket face to assist in lifting the ball over the net. This grip also disguises the player's intent and allows them to change the direction of the ball better than other grips. The player who uses this grip usually has a better backhand than forehand. CAUTION- this player is usually deadly with their drop shots.

Areas of Weakness:

1. This grip is not as popular as the other grips because it lacks power on certain strokes. It is particularly ineffective on balls that bounce chest high or higher.

2. You can rule out other shots such as topspin lobs and punishing approach shots. Because this grip does not hit topspin comfortably, you can forget about power off the ground stroke.

Question: How do you play against a Continental grip?

Answer: Hit heavy topspin to keep the balls bouncing up to the chest or higher on your opponent. Serve topspin serves to their forehand. Attack first; it is difficult for a Continental grip user to hit passing shots using a slice. Be a patient player!

Although it will not guarantee a win, looking at your opponent's grip in pre-match warm up may give you an opportunity to find a weakness in their game. Remember that losing can be a lesson in *your* weaknesses.

Stroke Styles and Where to Attack

Backswings

Bjorn Borg was the first user of the modern day *big* looping backswings. His strokes were considered radical at the time; however, they proved to be very effective. Many club players tried to duplicate his strokes but found they couldn't duplicate his effectiveness. If your strokes are working for you, then there is no need to change just because I pointed out soft spots in those strokes.

Every stroke has strength and every stroke has weakness. Let's start by reviewing the different backswings available. There is a straight swing and a loop swing.

The straight backswing—or flat backswing, as it is sometimes called—is most often taught to the beginning player because it is a simple stroke. It consists of turning the shoulders with the racket straight back. Because this stroke has fewer components, the player has less chance of making errors. This backswing is more adaptable to different or unexpected bounces. It also is a good stroke for doubles because of its short motion. Doubles typically have quicker exchanges, and the shorter motion of this swing allows you to be quicker to the contact point. In addition to its simplicity, it is harder for an opponent to read the direction intent of the stroke because of the lack of clues this backswing gives. Stroke deception is always strength. Proponents of the straight backswing say, *the less motion in a swing, the less that can go wrong with that swing.*

Areas of Weakness:

1. This swing does not lend itself to excessive spins and, therefore eliminates shots such as angling balls off the court and topspin lobs that require the excessive spin to execute properly.

DIAGNOSING WEAKNESSES

2. Balls that bounce chest high or higher. To oppose the high bouncing ball, you must hit up and across the ball. The straight backswing promotes more of a racket movement from beneath the ball and hits under the ball causing the ball to sail long. Additionally, as mentioned, the straight-back swing does not create very much spin on the ball and to handle excessive high bouncing balls, you must counter with spin.

3. This swing does not generate high racket velocity, particularly, if the back swing comes to a stop position behind the player. A "start, stop, start" motion losses its smoothness and its power.

4. The straight-back swing makes running for a wide ball awkward. If I were to ask you to turn and run without a racket in your hand you would use your arms for pumping to help you run faster. The straight-back swing makes it difficult to run with the racket extended behind you because your arms want to pump and help you get to the ball.

Question: How do you play against a straight backswing?

Answer: You hit excessive spin, preferably topspin, so the ball plays high in the hitting zone of your opponent. The straight-backswing player is normally an all-court player who will come to the net at the first opportunity. You should play the ball deep and get to the net at the first opening.

The loop backswing's circular motion is what many top-ranked players use. It is a continuous motion that generates high racket velocity. Topspin is its most comfortable spin but it does allow you to hit slice.

The loop motion starts with the shoulders and hips turned. Some players, like Pete Sampras or Andy Roddick, will lead back with the racket elbow, then raise the racket head above the hand while lowering his elbow closer to his body. Other players, like Roger Federer, will turn the shoulders and hips then lead back with the racket head while the racket elbow stays close to the body.

Areas of Weakness:

1. Wide balls. This is a stretching shot with the arm fully extended. The loop swing can not get under the ball sufficiently to lift it up over the net.

2. Control. Because of the perfect timing required in a loop backswing (timing defined as when the ball and the racket arrive in the contact zone at the same time), control can be a problem.

3. Wind and bad bounces can create hazards, since once the swing is started, the player can not easily adapt to last second changes.

4. Low, penetrating, bouncing balls often do not allow the player sufficient time to complete the loop.

Question: How do you play a loop swing?

Answer: Keep your balls bounces low—preferably, both low and angled. Approach with a slice, again, so the ball stays low and penetrates. Try to hit angle shots toward the sideline when you get into a ground-stroke rally. This will make your opponent hit on the full stretch. Serve wide to make them extend for the return. Another tactic is to constantly mix up your spin; hit slice and topspin at different times. This constant mix will prevent your opponent from getting into a rhythm on their strokes.

DIAGNOSING WEAKNESSES

Stroke Styles

One-Handed Backhand vs. Two-Handed Backhand

All teaching pros have their preference, one hand or two, and the discussion will continue long after this book. My position is there is no good or bad, just effective and ineffective.

The one-handed backhand has seen resurgence in popularity with the top touring pro due to its versatility. It can hit a slice effortlessly, topspin comfortably, and move in front of the body with ease.

Areas of Weakness:

1. The one-handed backhand feels weak at the early stage of learning tennis because a player needs time to develop the body strength needed to hit this stroke well.

2. The one-handed backhander must hit early because the shoulder that houses the racket arm is in front of the racket at the start of the swing. It is not until the racket is in front of the shoulder that the backhand feels strong enough to hit the ball over the net.

3. The most powerless feeling for a tennis player is when the ball bounces above shoulder height, particularly, for a one-handed backhand player.

Question: How do you play against a one-handed backhand?

Answer: Since the high backhand feels the most powerless, serve a high bouncing ball (kick serve) to the opponent's backhand. In a ground-stroke exchange, hit with a looping topspin that will bounce high to the backhand side. Because the backhand must be hit early, approach shots to the backhand side will often break down that one-handed side and cause a late-hit error.

The two-handed backhand has aided all levels of players—the beginner because of the instant strength that it presents in contrast to the one-handed, and the advanced tournament player because of the topspin that can be hit with comfort. It also helps the player disguise their shot selection especially well when hitting passing shots.

Areas of Weakness:

1. The two-handed player will be forced into a weak return, especially if the player does not let go with their left hand (or right hand if left-handed) on extremely wide shots. A ball placed extremely low and in front of a two-hander will force them to bend lower to the return the ball than a one-hander. A two-hander may also lack the maneuverability that is necessary to return an effective shot when a ball is hit extremely close to their body and jams the non-racket hand.

2. Balls that are hit at the extremities of the court. A two-handed backhander must be extra quick to counter the shots that are hit to the extremities.

3. Slice is an uncomfortable spin for this player. The left-hand (or right hand if left-handed) restricts the follow through needed to get depth on the stroke.

Question: How do you play the two-hander?

Answer: Serve wide to the backhand side or serve at the body to jam them. In ground-stroke rallies, hit a slice to keep the ball low. Keep the two-hander in a state of movement, never letting them have an opportunity to set up on the ball. Keep the ball out of their stroke zone.

To summarize, go through this checklist to exploit your opponents stroking style:

a.   Are they left- or right-handed?

b.   Do they take a loop backswing or straight backswing?

c.   Do they have a one-handed or two-handed backhand?

Answer these questions and then review what was discussed for weaknesses.

Playing Styles—Rock, Scissors, or Paper?

"For every style of play there is a way to attack,

for every attack there is a way to defend."

Remember the game "Rock, Scissor, Paper"? Rock beat scissors, scissors beat paper, and paper beat rock. Who is the winner? In tennis terms, each has indirect wins over the other. With that in mind, let's look at the three basic styles of tennis players. The aggressive (rock) player will try to overpower you. The baseline (scissors) player will try to carve you up with your mistakes. An all-court player (paper) is a complete player, one who can cover the baseline or the net. Let's examine each style and its traits.

The aggressive style (rock) player likes to initiate the attack. An attack-first individual, rock's strengths usually include a piercing serve, a good first volley, a good approach shot, and an equally good overhead. When those four strokes are "on," the rock is devastating.

Areas of Weakness:

1. There is no consistency with this type of player. They are either "on" and devastating, or they are "off," and equally devastated.

2. This player has no other way to play. Compare this to happily driving your car and everything is going along quite well. Then, boom, you have a flat tire and you discover you have no spare. What choices do you have? The aggressive (rock) player may be cruising along well in a match then, boom, their game goes flat and they have no spare style to play.

Question: How do you beat the aggressive player?

Answer: The best defense is a good offense, so get to the net before they do. When they attack first and come to the net, remember that rock does not perform well when pressured into making shot-selection decisions at the net. You should force them to decide hastily where to place the first volley. You can do this by dropping your shots below the net and forcing their volley to be hit up. Now, they must decide to go in front of you or behind you with their volley as shown in the diagram.

Stay mentally in the match even if the score is one-sided in favor of your opponent. Your "on" opponent may hit a flat segment at any time, and you

DIAGNOSING WEAKNESSES

must be prepared to recognize and seize that opportunity. The aggressive player often has trouble defeating the all-court player.

Being an all-court (paper) player, in many opinions, is the best way to play tennis. This player can attack or stay back. The strength of paper is that it has no weaknesses. A good all-court player such as Roger Federer has all the strokes of an aggressive player *and* a baseline player.

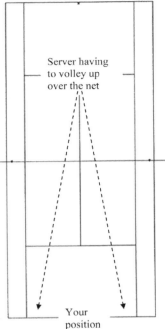

Areas of Weakness:

1. This style of play takes longer to develop because all strokes must be mastered.
2. Ignorance is bliss, as the saying goes. Because of the many options of the paper player, making quick decisions as to which style to play on which point and which shot to hit on each stroke can sometimes cause confusion. There's too much to think about in too little time.

Question: How do you play an all-court player?

Answer: This player normally attacks after they are given an invitation by a short ball. You can control their position by keeping the ball deep in the court and keeping them pinned to the baseline. The baseline style of play will give an all-court player the most trouble.

The baseline (scissors) player is the most frustrating player to play against. A baseliner will show you precisely where your weaknesses are by using the philosophy "I don't win matches, I let you beat yourself." You can expect good court coverage, good consistency, and sufficient depth in shot placement. Scissors players usually have a good understanding of the strategies and tactics of the game, plus excellent physical conditioning so they can run all day long.

Areas of Weakness:

1. The scissors player is like the aggressive player: what you see is what you get. If the baseline game is not working, they have no other way to play.

2. Baseliners have no danger zone on their side of the court. You can hit the short ball to this type of opponent and still be in a good position to win the point because a scissors player lacks attacking strokes.

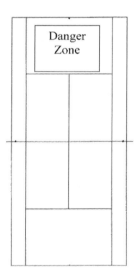

3. This style of player usually does not demonstrate adequate volley skills.

DIAGNOSING WEAKNESSES

Question: How do you play a baseliner?

Answer: You must play an aggressive style of tennis. Hit short balls to the corners to bring a baseliner up and out of the court. Another tactic is to hit drop shots to draw the baseliner off the baseline. Then depending on their shot selection, you choose your shot selection as shown in the diagram below.

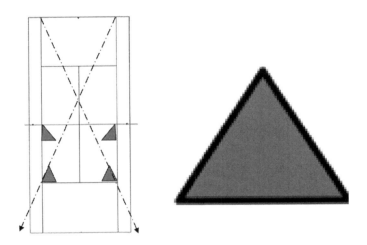

represents target areas

This brings us full circle with the different styles of play: rock beats scissors, scissors beats paper, and paper beats rock. You now have the tools to determine your own weaknesses and those of your opponent by analyzing stroke styles, playing styles, and grip differences. Keep delving until you find that weak link.

Scouting Report

So that you can apply all the information that has been presented to you, I have developed a scouting report form to help you figure out your upcoming opponents' strengths and weaknesses ahead of time. You can fill it out during idle time at tournaments.

Below is an example of a filled-in scouting report:

Name: Joe Smith   From: Carmel, CA.
Tournament: Easter Bowl "96"   Age Group: Boys 16's
Site: Rivera Resort   Surface: Hard
Round: 64   Date: 4/8/05
Left/Right: Right   Style of Play: Aggressive Baseliner
Best Stroke: Forehand   Weakest Stroke: Net Play

Forehand Grip: Semi-western   FH 1/2: 1   FH Backswing: Loop
FH Spins: Topspin   FH Soft Spot: low bouncing balls
Backhand Grip: Eastern   BH 1/2: 2   BH Backswing: Straight
BH Spins: Moderate topspin   BH Soft Spots: 1 handed slice
Serve Grip: Continental 1st Serve: Slice 2nd Serve: Kick
Unique Serving Characteristics: 1st serve can be powerful on occasion
Forehand Volley Grip: Eastern FHV 1/2: 1
FHV Soft Spots: Low
Backhand Volley Grip: Continental   BHV 1/2: 1
BHV Soft Spot: Not much penetration to volley

Pace: Deliberate   Demeanor: Outburst   Mental Game: Fighter

DIAGNOSING WEAKNESSES

Opponent's weaknesses—When hitting ground strokes, he doesn't handle low balls well. He has very little penetration on his one-handed backhand slice. He looks very uncomfortable around the net. His second serve will land short on important points.

Playing strategy—Hit balls wide to his forehand side, then come back to the backhand side in hopes that he will have to come off with his left hand to hit the one-handed backhand slice. When he does hit the one-hand be prepared to attack that response *with your strength*.

On important points when he has missed their first serve, change your receiving position to apply more pressure to his second serve.

When he is at the net, direct your passing shots to his backhand side.

Opponent's strength—His forehand is his weapon. If that ball sits up in front of him he will end the point. There is no quit in this player, when he is down in the match he gets tougher, more determined.

Observation—This match was won by Bob Jones 6–4, 7–6. It was a windy day, which seemed to bother Joe Smith more than Bob Jones.

CHAPTER 3

Applying Pressure

We assume, all too often, that there is only one way to apply pressure to an opponent: by hitting the ball harder. Next time, be extra attentive when watching the pros play, and you will see these players using five different ways to apply pressure. After reading this chapter, you should have a better understanding of how your play can pressure your opponent and how to get the result that you want: errors by your opponent. The pressures that we will be discussing are:

1. pace

2. power

3. spin

4. placement

5. position

Pace

What is it? How do you get it? How do you keep it? Pace, contrary to what many players think, does not mean power. Granted, power does result in a quicker pace, but having a faster pace does not make you a power hitter. Pace, by definition, is a rate of movement, performance, or occurrence. In tennis terms, pace can be how fast you move between points, which determines the frequency of the points, or pace can be how quickly you send the ball back to your opponent.

Let's discuss how quickly one moves between points. Much has been written and said about Rafael Nadel's slow, deliberate pace between points. He has done quite well with that slow pace, but every player is different. You and I may need a little less time between points to achieve our optimum playing speed. Studies have shown that most players feel comfortable playing in the sixteen-second range between the end of the last point to the start of the next point. To determine the best pace between points for you, have a friend use a stopwatch to time you the next time you play a match. Record the time between points and whether you won or lost the point. After the match, you may see a trend of when you are winning or losing points by the interval between points. You can use this information to determine the best pace of play for you. Remember, however, you still have to play within the boundaries of the United States Tennis Association's rule on time between points: "The receiver must play to the reasonable pace of the server and must be ready to receive when the server is ready to serve."

When necessary, there are several ways to slow down your opponent to match your level of pace: toweling off after each point, asking for the balls to be on your side of the court before you serve, or walking to pick up all the balls on your side of the court before you serve or receive. These tactics maybe construed as "gamesmanship" to your opponent, so make sure you are using them within the guidelines of the above-referenced USTA rule.

APPLYING PRESSURE

Pace, as noted, can also be how quickly you send the ball back to your opponent. You can regulate the pace of the point by standing inside or on the baseline. By doing this, you will get to the ball quicker and send it back to your opponent sooner at a pace they may be uncomfortable playing. A word of caution—when trying to hurry your opponent, you will also be hurrying yourself. Make sure your opponent is the one making the mistakes! You may want to go back and read the section titled "Take it on the Rise and Give Them a Surprise!" in chapter 1 (Curl's Pearls).

If moving inside the baseline picks up the pace of the point, then obviously moving farther back in the court can slow down the pace. The ball will take longer to get to you and you will take longer to return it. This is a good tactic to use if your opponent is hitting the ball harder than you want. More words of caution—when playing farther back in the court, you leave yourself open to your opponent's sharply angled shots.

Finally, you can change the pace of the point being played by changing the trajectory of the ball. The lower the trajectory, the quicker it will get to the other side. Conversely, the higher the arc, the longer the ball will take to get to the other side. Take advantage of changing the trajectory of the ball in the middle of a point to disrupt the rhythm of your opponent's strokes.

Power

Power—most players think that it is the *only* way to apply pressure to an opponent. In fact, as you will learn, it is just one of five possible ways. Power can be defined as the exertion of effort for a purpose. In tennis, the exerted effort is to make the ball travel at a greater velocity for the purpose of applying pressure to, and bringing about a mistake from, your adversary.

Every time you hit a ball, you are placing energy into that ball. That energy is either velocity (power) or rotation (spin). When applying velocity to the ball, you must make sure you understand how the power is generated: *the arm is control, the body is power.* The job of the arm is to position the racket at point of contact to put the ball where you want it to go. Power is generated when your arm does its job and, at the same time, you transfer your body weight forward and unwind your trunk (hips and shoulders) into the stroke. If this is done with the proper chain of body explosions, you will develop an effortless, controlled stroke. If you try to generate too much power by swinging the arm faster, with no assistance from the body, you will get power but lose control.

Still another way to put power on the ball is by using your opponent's energy. *Energy in, energy out.* For example, your opponent just hit a hard, fast-traveling serve. You put your racket out to meet the ball and your return is a blur right back into their court. What did you do to make the ball go back so fast? Nothing! Their power in, their power out.

What happens if your opponent hits with too much power? You return their shots with slice. Slice kills power.

Spin

There are two ways that a ball will find the court: gravity and spin. If you are not using spin then you are not playing at your full tennis-playing potential. Why do I say that? Spin lets you control the ball *after* it leaves your racket and when it is on your opponent's side of the court; and when the ball is in your opponent's court, spin will pose dilemmas for your opponent.

First, I want to destroy two myths about creating spin. Myth one: topspin is placed on the ball by hitting the ball and rolling the racket over the top of the ball. Myth two: slice is achieved by hitting the ball and rolling the racket face under the ball. Fact: whether hitting topspin or slice, the racket face is vertical at contact while the arm is traveling up, (topspin) or down

APPLYING PRESSURE

(slice) the back side of the ball to create the spin. Spin is *not* created by rolling the racket over or under the ball.

As I mentioned above, spin allows you to control the ball after it leaves your racket. What does the ball do after it leaves your racket? A ball will move through the air in the same direction it is rotating. If the ball is rotating forward and down as a result of topspin, the ball will move down into the court more quickly and, once it bounces, the ball will *explode* forward, giving your opponent less time to prepare for the shot. Depending on the trajectory of the ball, topspin will not only explode forward but the ball can rebound high above your opponent's shoulders forcing them to play the ball from a weak height disadvantage. A modern player who uses spin well is Rafael Nadal.

Furthermore, topspin will allow you to pull your opponent out of the court. According to Wimbledon Champion John Newcombe, "topspin changes the geometry of the game." By definition, geometry is the mathematics of relationships of points, lines, angles, surfaces, and solids; topspin allows players to hit with greater angles than would be possible without topspin.

Topspin can also provide you the shot-making capabilities to drop the ball at the short corners, which are the corners where the service line and singles lines meet. By hitting the ball to the short corners, you can draw your opponent off the court, thereby creating two options for your next shot: 1) hitting the ball to the open court, or 2) waiting for your opponent to run to the open court and then hitting behind them. These options are illustrated in diagram #1.

On the other hand, a ball rotating under and up (slice) takes a little longer to arrive over the net and, once it bounces, given its low trajectory, the ball will stay low. This low rebound can make it difficult for your opponent to return the ball with very much power since your slice ball stayed below the height of the net and out of their optimum stroke zone.

Slice forces your opponent to hit up and risk hitting the ball too hard and sending it long. A good time to use slice is when you want to slow down your opponent's power balls. *Slice kills power.* Likewise, killing their power may slow down the pace of the points to a tempo at which you can feel more in control.

To sum up, slice is a control spin with a slightly shorter stroke and a firmer wrist; topspin is a more aggressive spin with a longer stroke and a looser wrist. Additional information on how to use spins to neutralize the effects of the wind on the ball can be found in chapter 4, "Tricks of the Trade."

Placement

There are seven target areas as shown in the diagram to the right. These seven targets can be placed into three categories: deep, short depth, and opponent's weakness. These categories can be further broken down into descriptive tactics. As generally defined, a tactic is the art or skill of employing available means to accomplish a desired end. Below you will find different tactics or placements to accomplish your desired end.

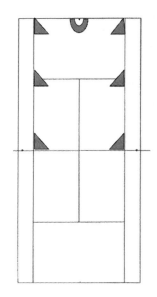

First, *deep*—Hitting the ball with depth will give your opponent more trouble than anything else that we have discussed in this chapter about applying pressure. Try this experiment on yourself. Have someone feed you three balls, all fed with the same velocity (power) but each one a little deeper than the next. After the three balls, ask yourself which one gave you the most

APPLYING PRESSURE

trouble. Your answer will probably be the deepest-landing ball. If it gives you the most difficulty, then it stands to reason that it will also give your opponent the same difficulty. Why? The deep ball does not give your opponent time to set up for the return and it can keep them off balance while they are hitting the stroke. Your opponent will also find it hard to mount an offense while they are in a defensive position on the court. You may want to refer to the earlier picture to see what I mean by deep targets.

Second, *short depth*—This may sound like a contradiction, but it is not. Each shot has an intended depth—some deep, some short. The short depth shot is designed to move your opponent up into the court to an area in which they are uncomfortable. Pulling an opponent with a weak volley up to the net by hitting a drop shot is a good use of the short depth. You will see in the diagram above that I also include the short corners as short depth. Hitting to the short corners is particularly effective against baseline players who want to stay at the baseline. Refer back to chapter 2, "Diagnosing Weaknesses"; in the section about styles of play you will see how the short-corner tactic can be used.

Third, *opponent's weakness*—Remember tennis players are only as good as their weaknesses. Once you discover the weakness of your opponent, at every opportunity you should hit the ball to their soft spot. Again, I refer you back to the "Diagnosing Weaknesses" chapter to help you find your opponent's weaknesses. Every tennis player has a weakness; you just have to find it before the match is over.

Finally, you may have noticed the seventh target in the middle of the baseline. I refer to the middle target as the "Borg Target." Bjorn Borg described his basic strategy as hitting everything cross-court until he got in trouble. When he got in trouble, he hit the ball deep and down the middle. By hitting the ball deep and down the middle, you give yourself more time to recover. But what's more important, you are not giving your opponent a direct angle to an open court. Next time you are in trouble, try the Borg Target.

Position

Where you position yourself on the tennis court will have a great deal to do with your strategy and tactics. First, you must know the difference between strategy and tactics: strategy is the overview of attacking an adversary; tactic is the employment of that strategy. Your strategy may be to serve and volley. Your tactic would be to serve to a target where your opponent will have the most difficulty returning the ball with power or good placement. In this situation, a good strategy coupled with the proper tactical maneuver, and ending the point with you in a proper court position, will win the point.

What determines your court position? Your strategy, if you are *acting*, not *reacting*. You must act on your strategy, not react to your opponent's strategy. Again, let's use the serve-and-volley strategy as an example. Your position at the net puts an immediate burden on your opponent. Simply by being at the net, you are forcing an offensive return, maybe even trying to force a winner. If you approach the net often during the match, your opponent must hit winners a large percentage of the time—a very exhausting way to have to win points. If your opponent does hit enough winners past you to win the match, find comfort in knowing that, as the BBC commentator Dan Maskell once said, "It's what they did right to win the match, not what you did wrong to lose the match."

Strategically, a good court position to play from is the baseline, especially if you are consistent with your strokes and with your foot speed. Rafael Nadal is a fine example of both consistency and foot speed. His excellent foot speed puts an extra strain on his opponents by forcing them to place their ball closer to the lines than they would normally be capable of or be comfortable with. He never beats himself with choosing poor shot selections or hitting the ball out of his control range.

APPLYING PRESSURE

One more way to add pressure to your opponent is with *their* court position. By concentrating on where you place your ball, you can maneuver your opponent to an area where they are the most uncomfortable. For example, if your opponent does not like to play at the net, your strategy is to bring them to the net and your tactic to accomplish this is a drop shot. You add pressure by exposing their deficiency in net play.

CHAPTER 4

Tricks of the Trade

"It's what you learn after you know it all that counts," according to baseball manager Earl Weaver. That is what this chapter is all about. When we learn the sport of tennis, we are taught the strokes, the strategy, and the tactics, all of which have been covered in this and other tennis publications. At times, there is a need to know how to handle certain "stopping stones" that occur in a match. In this chapter, I am going to discuss how to turn those stopping stones into "stepping stones." It's what happens *after* you learn the strokes.

Trick #1—When You Break a String During the Point

When you break a string during a point, run to the net. Most of us have heard, and some of us have had, a string break during a point. The sound of a broken string brings with it uncertainty about how the ball will play off your racket. This feeling of uncertainty is why you must end the point quickly and without conceding the point. Your best chance to win the point is to run to the net as soon as possible. By rushing the net at this time, you put the point-ending stroke on your opponent's racket, not yours (with the broken string). The result will be either they hit a winner or they will hit a loser, or you will hit a lucky winner. Two out of the three scenarios are good for you.

Trick #1A—When you break a string during a point and can't get to the net

Sometimes, you just can't get to the net because your opponent has hit the ball too deep for you to attack. If you have to rally with your opponent, shorten your strokes. The reason: the strings will lose a lot of tension as the point continues and with lower string tension, the result is more "fly" and more unpredictability from the racket. The shorter strokes will allow you some control on the ball.

Trick #1B—When your opponent breaks a string

When your opponent breaks a string, rush to the net on the next point. With unfamiliar and uncertain tension in their racket and with the pressure of you at the net, your opponent will find it most difficult to hit successful passing shots and will more than likely make a mistake.

Trick #1C

When you break a string, for the following point you should stay at the baseline and rally several shots, in order to get use to the new string tension. Ideally, all your rackets should feel the same. By feel I mean have the same balance, the same strings, and the same string tension. When you have your racket restrung, it's best to ask for the tension you like and have *both* rackets strung on the same stringing machine, as some stringing machines are calibrated differently. This will ensure that you have the same tension in both rackets.

TRICKS OF THE TRADE

Trick #2—Net Cord? Racket Up!

When you are at the net, many times you'll find that your opponent will make a passing attempt that will hit the top of the net, causing a net cord. When it hits the net, the ball will either 1) jump up high over your racket, called a "live" net cord or 2) trickle over the net, called a "dead" net cord. In either situation, put your racket up as soon as you realize the net cord. With your racket up, you can have a play on the live or dead net cords. For the ball that jumps up over your racket, your racket is ready—up and in front of the ball. For the one that dribbles over, you will have extra time to react because the trickle action takes more time to develop. An extra tip: a loose net means more net cords.

Trick #3—Wind Wisdom: Making the Wind Your Friend

In many areas of the country, players move from indoor tennis to outdoor tennis, from playing in conditions where weather isn't a factor to playing where the weather—specifically windy conditions—can wreak havoc with the ball flight.

We all dislike playing in windy weather conditions, but we have no control over the weather. The wind takes the ball in a direction we had not intended for it to go. But there are things you can do to counteract the influence of the wind on your shots and make your time playing in the wind a bit more enjoyable. And remember, the wind is a great neutralizer; it doesn't care if you're the number one seed or not. If you have a windy day and you're playing against a stronger opponent, the wind may play mayhem with the stronger player, neutralizing their strengths, and giving you a better chance for the upset.

Spin

With the Wind, Hit Topspin.

When the wind is at your back, gusting from behind you, the ball will carry farther than you intend. To counter this and to keep your shots from landing long on your opponent's side, you need to put more topspin on the ball. Topspin will work against the effect the wind has on the ball by pulling it down into the court.

Position

Wind in Your Face, Give Plenty of Space.

Wind at the Back, Depth the Opponent's Shot Will Lack.

When the wind is in your face, your opponent's shot will be coming at you more deeply and quickly. Positioning yourself farther back will give you more time to "read" where his or her shot will land.

Conversely, when the wind is at your back, you will need to position yourself closer to the baseline. Your opponent's shots will be "butting" up against the oncoming wind, resulting in a shorter landing ball on your side. By positioning yourself closer to the baseline you will not find yourself charging at the ball at the last instant.

Cross-Court Winds

Down the Middle Solves the Riddle.

When you are playing in a cross-court wind, it becomes difficult to calculate the effect the wind will have on the ball flight, particularly when hitting down the line. So as to not worry about the wind's effect on the ball, aim for the middle of the court. You'll increase your margin of error and give the ball more room to land in your opponent's court, rather than risk it going wide.

Serve

Power vs. Spin When Playing in the Wind

Here are a few tips when serving on windy days:

- Lower your ball toss—the wind plays havoc with ball tosses. To give the wind less opportunity to move your service toss around, don't toss the ball as high as you normally would.

- When serving into the wind, don't waste your energy attempting to deliver power on the serve. The wind in your face will kill the power.

- When serving in a cross-court wind, go with the wind. If the wind is blowing from right to left then spin the ball to where the wind will assist the movement of the ball.

Shot Selections

Touch Shots are Tough Shots

When attempting touch shots, lobs, or drop shots on windy days, you must know the direction from which the wind is gusting. A touch shot doesn't have power, so the ball won't cut through the wind, which allows the wind to have more influence on the flight. A few coaching tips:

- *Drop shots:* A good drop shot will be a bad drop shot when the wind is at your back. With the wind gusting from behind you, the ball will be carried deeper into the opponent's court than you planned, making it easier for the opponent to react and get to your shot. But when the wind is gusting in your face, a bad drop shot will be a good drop shot, because the wind will stop the ball more quickly and drop it into the court, making it land shorter, closer to the net. For the same reason, if the wind is a cross-court wind, then drop shot into the wind.

- *Lobbing into the wind:* It is important to feel the strength of the wind in your face to know how hard to hit your lob. My advice is not to be afraid to hit the lob out—give the shot enough power and know that the wind will keep it in the court.

- *Lobbing with the wind:* Again, it is important to know the strength of the wind behind you. A strong wind will require you to make the trajectory of the ball go straight up and let the wind carry it to the opponent's court. In short, you don't send it forward; you let the wind do that.

Trick #4—Heavy Weather Conditions

Most of us are asked to play matches in less-than-desirable weather conditions. As mentioned above, the wind can be one of those conditions.

TRICKS OF THE TRADE

Another common problem is having to play during a little rain, or on a court that is still damp from rain. These conditions are called heavy conditions. By absorbing some of the moisture on the court ("napping up"), the balls become heavier and larger.

Under these heavy conditions you should:

1. Think drop shot. Since the balls are heavier, they will give less bounce and give your opponent less time to read, react, and reach the ball.

2. Put your power game away. Remember, the balls are heavier and the courts are still moist. Those two elements will kill your power. The ball will move through the air more slowly, and the moist court will slow the ball down after it bounces.

3. Find the ball that best suits your strategy for the upcoming point. This sounds strange but as the balls become heavier, you might want the points to be played more slowly. In that case, find the balls that are the heaviest and have the most nap. On the other hand, if you want the points to be played faster then find the newer, less-used balls. They will be lighter and have less nap on them. Notice the touring pros when

they are playing. They ask for more than two balls from the ball boy when he is serving. This is to choose a ball that may be used less and give a quicker flight to their serve.

Trick #5—What to Choose When You Win the Toss

At the start of each match, I strongly recommend that, *before* the warm up period starts, there is a spin or toss of the racket to determine opening options. The winner of the toss gets to choose one of four options. I found that some tennis players do not realize that they have four options from which to choose, nor do they know the benefits. Below, I will go through each of the four options and explain the benefits.

Choice #1: Serve first. You should elect to serve if you have a good serve. You can count on winning your serve, thereby gaining the mental advantage by being one game ahead of your opponent. Match situation: You serve the first game and hold serve. You are up one–love. Your opponent serves, they hold. Score is one–all. You hold serve again; you go up two-one. Can you see the mental advantage to which I am referring? If you hold serve each time, you will always be one game up and your opponent should be struggling to hold serve just to even up the score.

Choice #2: Receive first. You can choose to receive serve first when you need the extra game time to warm up prior to your serve, as well as time, if needed, to calm your nerves.

Another advantage of receiving first is in the changeover. Follow this closely: You choose to receive first, your opponent serves and holds; one–love. Because the next game is an odd game, you switch sides, and you get 90 seconds to sit down and towel off before going to serve. You hold serve, and then your opponent serves and holds. The score is two–one in games, an odd-game

TRICKS OF THE TRADE

total. You go sit down, towel off, and then go to serve. Can you see what is happening? Before each one of *your* service games, you get to sit down, towel off, relax, and then serve. Your opponent, on the other hand, must go immediately into the serve after the final point of your serve game.

Choice #3: Select a side of the court. You want to choose a side mainly because of the sun or wind. When choosing a side, take into consideration the position of the sun. You want to avoid looking into the sun on your first service game, and instead, force your opponent to stare into the sun on their first service game. When choosing sides based on wind direction, you want to serve with the wind because it is easier to hold serve. Why? With the wind's help your serve will penetrate farther and, if everything holds true to form, you will be serving at four–four in the set with the wind once again at your back. Another tip when serving with the wind is to toss the ball farther into the court than you would normally do. This will help bring the ball down into the court and not allow the wind to carry it long. When serving against the wind, remember, your energy will be wasted hitting the ball with power because the oncoming wind will kill any power.

Choice #4: Defer—let your opponent decide. That's right, if you win the toss, you can waive the decision to your opponent. You might want to do this if the sun or the wind is a major factor. You win the toss and you opt to defer the decision to your opponent, who chooses to serve. You can then choose which side of the court you want and avoid looking into the sun. If you must serve, you can pick the side with the wind at your back for your first service game. Finally, your opponent can choose a side and you get a choice between whether to serve or to receive. In most scenarios, you can arrange it so that the sun and wind benefit your game rather than your opponent's. Plus, by choosing to defer you receive two choices, 1) the choice to defer and then 2) after the opponent makes a choice you get to choose the option that is left over.

Trick #6—Miss-hits? Hit Them!

Sometimes in a match you can hear the sound of the ball hitting your opponent's frame and the ball is still making its way over to your side of the court. This is called a miss-hit and miss-hits are very difficult to handle. Neither you nor your opponent can take a good guess at the direction the ball will take after it bounces. The best option to choose when facing a miss-hit is to take the ball out of the air. By taking the ball out of the air, you eliminate the direction the ball would have bounced.

Another occasion when you must be ready to return a miss-hit is when you are at the net. You are positioned at the net; your opponent miss-hits the passing shot. The height of the ball looks like it will land out, so you leave it. Unfortunately, the ball falls in due to the miss-hit shot's heavy dose of spin. A miss-hit ball will find the court more times than not, so when your opponent miss-hits a passing shot, don't leave it, hit it!

Trick #7—Drop Shots: Focus, Frantic, or Fatigue?

You can learn much about the mental state of the person on the other side of the net when your opponent attempts a drop shot from a poor court position. Are they confident, desperate, or tired? First, let's discuss confidence.

Focus: When you are behind in a match, your opponent may feel confident and may mentally check out. By checking out, they may try some inopportune drop-shots, such as when they are behind the baseline or at an important point in the game. They may feel they have a commanding lead, forget about some of the basic principles of drop shots, and attempt to hit them anyway. If your opponent is doing this, now is the time to climb back into the match because they have probably lost their focus.

Frantic: A player who hits a drop shot from a poor position in the court may be showing signs of desperation. *Desperate people seek desperate measures.* If your opponent is behind in the match or in trouble during a point, they may try to turn the score around with a great shot, a drop shot. When you see this happening, realize that your opponent may be frantic. You can deliver the knockout blow by focusing on the next few points, by playing the points smart, and by not giving your opponent any cheap (quick) points in their favor.

Fatigue: Your opponent may need to end the points quickly because they are physically spent; fatigue has set in. Look for tiredness as a sign of why your opponent tries a drop shot.

In all three situations—focus, frantic or fatigue—you should know what is really being broadcast: the condition of your opponent is unsound.

Finally, I should emphasize that drop shots are an integral part of any strategy in tennis. I am not suggesting that you should not attempt drop shots. Rather, I'm giving you this information to let you know about what you can read between the lines when your opponent attempts a drop shot at a tactically poor time or in a tactically poor position.

Trick #8—Put-Aways and Why They Get Away

Picture this: your opponent puts up a short floater and, recognizing that they left an open court for you, you come charging in and...blow it! Sound all too familiar? Well, if you find comfort in knowing that you are normal, then you are normal. No matter whether you are a beginner or a touring pro, you will eventually miss a "sitter." But why? I see one of three common mistakes when this miss occurs. The player is too anxious, too casual, or too greedy. Which one were you?

1. Being too anxious usually happens when you see that your opponent has left open an area of the court. You want to get the ball to that opening before your opponent has an opportunity to recover and close down the open court. When rushing or being too anxious with the stroke you tend to hit off balance and then the mistake happens.

2. Being too casual about the stroke commonly happens when you know you have the opening and a easy put-away, but then you fail to make it to the ball while it is still at a good put-away height, usually when it is above the net. Another manifestation of being too casual is being too careful. By not wanting to make a mistake you tend to hit the ball too easy or place it too much in the center of the court. Both mistakes will allow for the opponent to recover.

3. Being too greedy is the most common reason that players miss the easy shots. Greedy players are inclined to hit the ball harder or closer to the line than is necessary to win the point. In Allen Fox's book, *Winning Tennis,* he states that "there are no three-point plays in tennis." Whether you hit the ball off the line at 110 mph for a winner or hit the ball five feet from the line at 70 mph to win a point, the point value is the same—one. Never hit a ball harder or closer to the line than necessary to win each point.

Finally, some good news. All the reasons for missing the easy sitters are emotional. They have nothing to do with your stroke mechanics. You need not worry that your strokes are poor if you can keep your emotions in check.

Trick #9—Rules of Opposing Styles

You will face many different opponents; some will be aggressive, some will be consistent, and some will be cute. Different playing styles pose different

TRICKS OF THE TRADE

problems and require different solutions. I will explore the aggressive, consistent, and cute playing styles and discuss how best to neutralize each one.

Rule #1: *You beat an aggressive player by playing aggressively first.* By aggressive, I mean a player who will come to the net quite often or hit punishing ground strokes. They are always practicing their offensive style, while neglecting their defensive skills, i.e., passing shots, lobs, etc. Since they don't practice those defensive skills, then you must make them play the style of tennis that requires them to hit those shots. To do this, you must play offensive tennis before they do.

Rule #2: *You don't push with a pusher nor bang with a banger.* First, an explanation of a "pusher" and "banger." A pusher is a player who just gets the ball back into play; they rely on their consistency and your mistakes to beat you. A banger is a person who relies on their power to beat you.

When things are going your way in a match setting, there is no reason to shop around for another game plan. But often, if things aren't going your way, you must look for another strategy. First, ask why the game isn't going your way. Are they a better pusher than you? Or are they a better banger than you?

Let me pose these questions differently. If you were fighting against a heavyweight boxing champion who likes to knock out his adversaries quickly, would you go toe-to-toe with him when you know he punches harder than you do? Of course not! Well, that is what a banger does to you. He wants you to match punches with him.

Conversely, the pushers do not hit with power. Rather, they hit and run and hit and run, hoping you will get frustrated by the constant returns and make mistakes by attempting to hit the ball too close to the line or hit too hard when you are not in a good position, or that eventually you will push with them so that they will have you playing their style of tennis—not yours. *Don't push with a pusher nor bang with a banger.*

Rule #3: *Don't get cute with someone who's cuter than you.* By "cute" I mean a player who likes to drop shot, lob, and "dink" the angles. When playing against a cute player you get lulled into playing their style of tennis by trying to get cute yourself, using drop shots or lobs when you normally don't play that way. In short, they bring us *down* to their level.

You need to keep this cute player back deep, or off the court, moving them away from the net. Place them in an area of the court where their cute play won't be effective. And stay focused. It is very easy to lose your concentration against this person and let up. Before you realize it, you are playing their cute style of tennis. *Don't get cute with someone who's cuter than you.*

Trick #10—Breaking Serve, Think First and Third

When watching a tennis match, we often hear the commentator refer to "breaking serve," or "break point." Breaking serve is when the receiver wins the game the opponent is serving. Break point refers to the point in the game score when, if the receiver won that particular point, they would have broken (won) the game their opponent is serving.

To help break serve, you must change the way you look at the first and third points in each game. The conventional plan for the receiver is to work into the game, since the first point in each game does not pose any immediate loss. That type of thinking makes for a great many lost opportunities to break serve. With regard to the third point, the receiver doesn't feel the sense of emergency, or the importance, in the point, so they may play a relaxed point.

I contend that the first point in the server's game is the key to breaking serve. It has been proved that the first point in each game determines the

TRICKS OF THE TRADE

attitude of the participants. If the server wins the first point, they gain confidence and can leave the receiver thinking, "I'll give their serve game to them and concentrate on winning my serve game." If the receiver wins the first point, statistics show that the receiver's chance of breaking serve goes up from 25% to 50%—a real opportunity for the receiver to break serve, because the server knows that this game is in a little danger of being lost. Additionally, if as the receiver you win the first point, you know you can apply more pressure to the serve.

An example of this type of pressure on an opponent occurred in the finals of Wimbledon in 1996, when MaliVai Washington played Richard Krajicek. The first set ended at 6–3 Krajicek; in the second set, it was 4–all, with Washington serving. The first point was won by Krajicek. Knowing that he was up 0–15 so he could apply more pressure to Washington's serve, Krajicek hit his return-blazing cross-court for an outright winner. Now Krajicek was up 0–30, just two points from breaking serve with an opportunity to close out the set. The pressure was then squarely on Washington.

Would Krajicek have been so aggressive with his return if he was down 15–0? And even if he had been and the results were the same, the score would have just been 15–15. Quite a different feel to the receiver's game of 15–15 as opposed to 0–30, don't you think?

The third point is important to breaking serve, because it's a transport point. It can transport you to break point or to an even score. For example, it's 15–30 (third point). The server wants to win the point to even the score at 30–30, but their service game is still in contention. The receiver wants to win the point to take them to double break point, 15–40; pressure is with the server. The receiver now has two chances to win one point and can take a little more risk in their shots. A rip from the hip!

Breaking serve, think first and third.

Trick #10 – It's Not a Break Until You Hold

To win a match, it is critical that you break your opponent's service game some time in each set. If each player holds serve, (each player winning their service games) then each set comes down to a tie-breaker, so you can see how you must hold serve while breaking serves to win the set and the match.

There are two parts to breaking serve. The first is the breaking of serve (winning the service game of your opponent), which we just discussed in Trick "9". The second part is the holding of serve (winning your service game). To capitalize on the break of serve that you just worked so hard to accomplish, you must now focus on holding serve. What you do *not* want to do is relax after the break and then get broken right back. To prevent that, the idea is to win the first point in your service game. By winning that first point and by breaking serve in the previous game, your opponent may show signs of discouragement.

What happens if you *do* get broken? The thought is that the easiest time to break serve is immediately following the serve game in which you were broken. Your opponent may relax and perhaps play some loose points early in their service game.

To summarize—you must break serve to win a match, but to capitalize on that break you must hold serve.

You must consolidate your break with a hold.

Trick #10a—0–0 is the best time to be broken

If there is a best time to have your service broken, then the first game of each set is that time. I'm not giving you the go-ahead to lose your service game, but I am attempting to offer a positive outlook on losing an early service game.

Most players consider losing an early service game to be an indication of things to come. They generally think, *I just got out here and I'm already losing.* The positive viewpoint is *I'd rather be broken at 0–0 than at 4–all!* Why? If you lose your service early in a set, you have the rest of the set to get the break back. There is no urgency to break back, and you know that your opponent could have a physical or mental letdown at some time during the set. Anticipate and look for the opportunity to get the service break back.

As the set gets closer to a conclusion, every service game and every point has more consequences to the outcome. Therefore, if it's 4–all and I am broken, the score is 5–4 and my opponent is serving for the set or match. In that case, I *must* secure a break of serve to stay in the set or match; this is a real emergency state. In fact, at that moment in a match, you are not likely to get any letdown from your adversary because they know how close they are to finishing you off.

Trick #11—Rain Delays and How to Respond

If you play in tournaments, at some point you will have rainy days that cause a delay. How you respond to those delays or suspension of play can affect your performance. There are three types of rain delays: short rain delay, long rain delay, and suspension of daily scheduled play. I'm going to answer some questions that pop up about rain delays and how to respond to them. The most common questions are: Do you eat? What do you eat? Do you stay at the site?

First, let's talk about short rain delays. You are at a tournament; you are on court and your match just started when a light rain begins and play is halted. The tournament director requires that players stay on site because this may be a short rain delay (two hours or less). The first thing you should do is make sure you and your opponent agree on the game and set score, plus what side of the court you each were on. Then you and your opponent should report the score and which side you were on and return the balls to the tournament director. This procedure is important in preventing confusion, so that when you are called back to resume play, you continue with the correct score and on the same side as when you stopped play.

The next step is to put on a warm-up garment or sweater in order to keep your muscles from getting stiff. Go off with your coach or parent, or by yourself, to do some stretching. Again, this is to keep your muscles from getting stiff. If possible, stay outside, because clubhouses are usually air conditioned. While stretching, you may want to review your game plan with your coach or parent. If you were far enough into the match, you may want to adjust some tactics that were not working. A few words of caution: have your coach or parent keep the suggestions to a minimum, maybe two or three. Studies have proved that players can only retain one or two coaching suggestions, so more may only fog the mind. Finally, since the rain delay had thrown off your eating clock and you ate assuming that your match would be over at a projected time, eat a light snack, such as a bagel or some fruit.

When the tournament director announces that play will resume, say, in fifteen minutes, you need to get your adrenaline pumping again. Pull out the jump rope from your racket bag (if you don't have a jump rope, get one) and jump for five to ten minutes. Then review any game plan and return to your court. You will be given the same tennis balls you played with before the rain delay (USTA rules) and the tournament director will tell you how much time you have to warm up, usually five to ten minutes.

A long rain delay (two or more hours) poses some of the same problems, which have some of the same solutions as stated above. When you are called off the court, use the same procedures—confirm the score and sides with

TRICKS OF THE TRADE

your opponent, report this information to the tournament director, stay warm, stretch, and review your game plan with your coach or your parent. When the bad news comes from the referee that play has been suspended—but the tournament director wants you to check back in two hours to see if you can restart your match—go back to your hotel and eat. When you are unsure of how long it will be until you're back on court—but you know it will not be sooner than two hours—since you do not know when you will be able to eat again, now is the time to eat a *sensible* meal.

You will notice that eating is one of the main activities I mention on both the short and long rain delays. The reason that some players start to feel dizzy when they resume a delayed match is that the delay has thrown off their body clock, and their body needs fuel. When you check to see when the matches will continue, allot enough time to start your pre-match rituals of stretching, jumping rope, and reviewing your game plan.

The final rain delay is a suspension of play for the entire day—a rain out. Follow the procedures for reporting the score, and go back to the hotel and eat. Because each player deals with this type of delay differently, you should know how you perform best to determine how to spend your time during this rain suspension. If you feel the most confident about your game when you hit every day, have your coach/parent find an indoor facility and go hit with your coach or your parent, or have a hitting session with the club professional. If you find it more relaxing to have the day off from hitting, you may want to go to a movie or to the local mall. I recommend that if you take a day off from hitting, find the exercise room at the hotel and get someone to work out with you. (I know my body definitely needs the work out.)

Remember that in each rain delay, you should report the score, put on a warm-up suit, stretch, and eat, and then prepare to resume play, whether it is by jumping rope, engaging in your pre-match rituals, or going to a movie.

TENNIS: PLAY SMARTER NOT HARDER II

Trick #12—Regripping? A Penny for Your Thoughts.

Whether you're first learning to serve, or you've played for some time, one of the most frustrating things to learn is the grip. The teaching professional will move you from a comfortable eastern forehand to the uncomfortable—but necessary—continental grip. You may find it difficult to keep the continental grip, because it makes you feel weak when you hold on to the racket. There is a common problem called regripping, where you start with a continental grip but somewhere in the swing you regrip the racket in your familiar, stronger-feeling grip, usually an eastern forehand. Try as you might, your muscle memory (habits) changes the grip.

Here is a trick that has worked for many players.

Place a penny on the index finger knuckle pad, as shown in the picture. Grip the racket with the continental grip as you hold the penny against the handle. Serve, attempting to hold the penny against the handle.

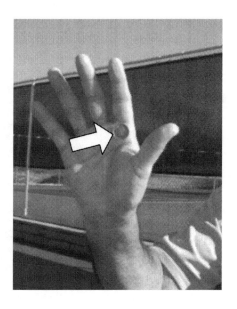

TRICKS OF THE TRADE

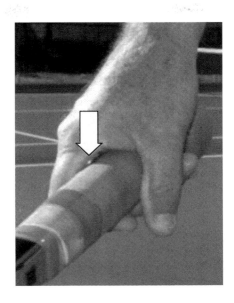

Two things may happen. Either you will keep the continental grip throughout the entire swing, which is what we want, or you will become aware when and where in your service motion you attempt to regrip the racket because you will drop the penny.

That's my two cents worth.

CHAPTER 5

Curlyisms

Great Shots Win Points, Good Shots Win Matches

Many times I observe tennis matches where the participants seem to be playing another game called "Who Can Hit the Most Spectacular Shot of the Match." Tennis is *not* about who can hit the most spectacular shot. As a matter of fact, when you study matches, you will see that generally, the player who sets up the points is the one who eventually wins the point.

Great shots may win you a point—and probably several points—in a match, plus a few oohs and aahs from the spectators, but that is all they will do. Good shots will win your match because all players are capable of hitting many goods shots per match. Again—study a touring pro match and you will see that even at their level of play, they hit mostly good shots and few great shots.

Next match, let your opponent hit the great shots. You hit the good shots and win!

TENNIS: PLAY SMARTER NOT HARDER II

Tennis Players Are a Bunch of Losers

That's a harsh statement, but it's true. Watch a tennis match at your club or park. Nine out of ten points are lost, not won. Players are trying to fire off winners from all parts of the court. This may bring some winners, but mostly losers.

Why? Other ball sports—football, basketball, soccer— train us to think, *If you have the ball, you should be offensive-minded. If you don't have the ball, you're defensive-minded.* Tennis is a unique ball sport. Those rules don't apply. Just because you are hitting the ball doesn't mean you're on offense, and conversely, because your opponent is hitting the ball doesn't mean you're on defense. But the prevailing notions of other ball sports have been ingrained in us. They come through when we are hitting the ball too aggressively and hit a losing shot.

Be a winner by *not* hitting winners. Let your foe be the loser.

Progress Today Determines Tomorrow's Achievements

When you take a tennis lesson, the instructor usually works on one of two things: eliminate a weakness from your game (so your opponent has nothing to attack) or give you a new stroke to strengthen your game. In short, either they're taking away or adding something to your game. Each can be discouraging, particularly if you cannot see the benefits that either of them will give you in the future.

As you learn a new stroke, you need to realize it will take time for you to feel comfortable and confident about how and when to use it. Remember— competence breeds confidence. Understanding and executing are two different concepts. You may understand what the instructor is teaching you, but execution is the difficult part.

If you are discouraged, keep in mind that what you work on today will pay off in the future. Progress today determines tomorrow's achievements.

Expect with Respect

You're told to project a positive image on the court but to not be overly arrogant. What's the difference? Where is the line between confidence and arrogance?

You should walk into every match willing to give it your all and expecting to win. But you also need to know that, although you maybe playing well, if your opponent is having a career day, you have no control over it. Respect the fact that your opponent may have their best day ever or that they have every capability to win the match, just as you do. As I quote in another part of this book, "Sometimes it's not what you did wrong; it's what your opponent did right."

So the invisible line from confidence to arrogance that I have spoken of happens when you expect to win *without* respect for the adversary. So my advice is: Be confident, not cocky. Expect to win. Have respect for the adversary.

Failure is an Event...Not a Person

We *all* lose. There are far more losers than winners in this sport. In the US Open tournament, there are 128 participants, and you will find only one player who did not lose a match, which means that 127 players lost.

When you lose, you may feel bad about your performance and think about all you could have done better to win. The only bad that comes from losing is when you do not learn something from it or when you take it too personally. Do not think for a moment that losing a tennis match says anything about you as a person. "Losing is not the end of the world...nor winning place you on top of it."

Learning Occurs When...

"I can't think and hit the ball at the same time!"

When I am teaching a new stroke, I often hear the frustration of my students in that comment. I agree with that statement. However, learning can only happen when first you think about a change in your stroke. *If it doesn't feel strange, then there's no change.* Now, it should feel different, but it should not hurt. Then with the feel that you acquired from the lesson, you must go out and own that stroke through repetition. The adage *Repetition is the mother of learning.* That adage is absolutely true in tennis. As the new conscious thought (change) you are incorporating into your game moves to an unconscious thought and becomes part of your stroke through repetition, you develop what is commonly known as a habit. This is how I find learning occurs in tennis.

Don't Let What's Going Wrong Get in the Way of What's Going Right

"I can't hit a forehand!," "My backhand stinks." "I can't buy a first serve," Have you made these statements to yourself lately? These are all comments we hear from players telling us what's *not* working. They dwell so much on what's going wrong with their game they give little thought to finding out what's going right. The result is that the whiner almost always loses the match.

In every long tennis tournament, you will probably have one day when you are not playing your best tennis. Since this sport of tennis is one in which the winner goes on and the loser goes home, you have to search for and discover a way to win that match. I recommend that you look for the strokes or strategies that *are* working for you. For example, you are normally a baseline player and today your ground strokes are not working but your serve is on. So, today you must win with a serve and volley strategy.

Champions find a way to win even when they are not playing their best tennis. They find it by looking at what *is* working for them and not dwelling on what *isn't* working for them. In other words, find a way to win with the cards that you are dealt.

Points are Won and Lost Well Before They're Won or Lost

Very rarely is a point over with just one swing of the racket; the service ace is the only exception. Typically, observers just witness the ending stroke, not the strokes building up to the end.

When watching or even playing a tennis match, note there is a beginning, middle, and end in each point played. It is the middle of each point I want you to be aware of, because points are won or lost in the middle.

During the middle of the point, a player will hit a shot that moves the adversary into a weakened position on the court, drawing a frail response. It is at that juncture that the complexion of the rest of the point changes till the point is won, usually by the person who forced the weak response.

Each point is won or lost well before the ending stroke. Be aware of the middle of the point and recognize the *beginning of the end*.

Go Through the Strength to Open Up the Weakness

Often your opponent will hide their weakness from you by running around their weakness to hit their strength. The phrase "running around" in tennis terms means that when you hit the ball to your opponent's weaker stroke (the backhand, for example), they will try to avoid returning the ball with their weak stroke by sprinting so far over to their weaker side that they're now in a position to hit with their strength (a forehand).

Another time that your opponent may run around is when they are trying to hit the off-forehand or the inside-out forehand. This type of forehand is your opponent's weapon, and they are trying to either end the point or at least start dictating the point with this stroke. Why hit a weakness when you have time to hit your strength? Roger Federer and Rafael Nadel are two examples of players who use this off-forehand tactic.

In both situations, when your opponent runs around, they are exposing more than half of their court to you and you should take what they give you. Hit the ball to the open court, which pulls your opponent to that side. Now you've opened up their weakness so you can direct the next stroke towards their weakness. Go through the strength to open up the weakness.

A word of caution: if you are going to hit to the strength of your opponent, make sure your shot is making them stretch out to hit the ball or this tactic may boomerang on you.

Winning Breeds Complacency

A tennis coach often encounters resistance when a player wants to try things their way rather than the coach's way. When this happens, and discussions have reached an impasse, the coach can either insist that the student does it the way they want or wait for the player to try it their way. After a time, players usually understand that coaching is designed to save them time and losses. To illustrate what I mean, read below about the boxer and his trainer and their different views on performing.

I watched a boxing match on TV. After the match was over, the commentator, as usual, interviewed the winning boxer's trainer. One of the questions directed to the trainer was, "How do you think your fighter performed?" The trainer responded, "He needs more work on his right hook." The winning boxer standing nearby heard this and said, "Yeah, but I won!" Without hesitation, the trainer looked back at his boxer and said, "So do you have to lose before you listen?"

That is one of the best statements I've heard in sports. This trainer realized his fighter was getting complacent about his boxing skills because he was winning. Too much time can be wasted waiting for a student to try things their own way before realizing their coach was right. Why was the coach right? Most likely the coach, a former boxer, tried the same thing the student was trying now with the same results. *A wise person learns from their mistakes, a wiser person learns from someone else's mistake* (Unknown).

You Get What You Give

This saying has several meaning to me, one that directly pertains to tennis and the other that pertains to life. Since this book is a book on tennis, I'll relate it to tennis.

1. Question: at all levels of play, who moves the least amount around the court? The touring pros? No. The SENIORS! Watch a doubles match when the participants are seniors. They hit the ball and then move into position for their opponents' most likely reply. What do they know you don't? They know that if you hit an angle shot to your opponent, you better guard against an angle reply. For example, you just hit one of

your best serves pulling your opponent out of the court. You got him, or so you think! Amazingly, they respond with an even better angle shot that pulls you farther out of the court than you pulled them. Your opponent was able to do this because they know when you give them an angle they can return with an angle. You Get Back What You Give; that is what the seniors know that you need to learn.

2. As a tennis coach, I am always amazed when a player plays a match with an effort level nowhere close to 100 percent. Then, when they come off the court, they complain they were not playing their best tennis. Why would anyone expect a 100 percent performance if the effort level was not an equal percentage? If you give 50 percent, expect 50 percent results; if you give 100 percent, expect 100 percent.

You get back what you give.

It's Not What You Did Wrong; It's What Your Opponent Did Right

I maintain that tennis players look for reasons to get down on themselves, particularly, when things aren't going their way. Your opponents will give you enough negative feedback by letting you know your mistakes, e.g., out, wide, fault, long, no! You don't need to heap more negatives on yourself. Granted, in tennis more points are lost by errors than are won by winners, but when your opponent does hit a winner, give them credit and keep your self-talk positive.

Tennis players are too quick to beat themselves up after losing a point. They always think they are at fault when they lose the point, but sometimes it isn't their fault. After you lose a point, stop and replay it in your mind. Did you do something wrong or could you have corrected something to stop your opponent from winning the point? If not, then relax and realize that it's *what they did right, not what you did wrong.*

CURLYISMS

The same mental approach can be used after you have lost a match. Replay the match in your mind and ask whether you gave your best effort. Did you hit your shots? Did you try different styles of play to confuse your opponent? If you answered yes to these questions, then again, I echo, it's not what you did wrong; it's what they did right.

Big Points Don't Mean You Have to Hit Big Shots

Here's one situation: It is 30–40, four games all, third set. You are serving a *big* point. What type of serve would you play? How about flat down the middle for an ace? And another: It's 15–30, three-four in games, first set. If you win this point, it is 30–all, but if you lose this point, you are down 15–40 with double break point for your opponent. Do you hit a big (hard) shot at the opponent? *Be honest.*

All players will find themselves in those kinds of situations and, invariably, we will feel the need to hit a big shot to get out of a big predicament. Alas, without fail, we often lose the point and dig a deeper hole to climb out of. Never hit a shot harder than you have to.

The answer to both of the above scenarios is to play aggressive but high-percentage strokes to apply pressure to your opponent. For instance, on the serve, 75 percent of your power directed at the weaker side or right at the opponent would apply pressure as well as a high-percentage shot.

Keeping your cool is tough in those situations. You must show what I call your "tennis maturity." I define tennis maturity as making the correct shot selections in pressure situations with a relaxed body. The above is summed up in the title: *big points don't mean you have to hit big shots.*

Are There Big Points in Tennis?

If you were to count the number of points won by each player in a match, the player who won the most points would be the victor nine out of ten times. If that is the case, every point has the same importance, and if you win more than the opponent you win the match. So, there are no big points. Each point is the same.

Now, add one human trait to the mix: *emotion*. Emotion is what makes big points. After losing a point, players tend to get down on themselves, letting their emotions get the best of them, which may even result in still more points being lost. That one point was so big it won two or three points—for the opponent. To solve this, the player should control their emotions and not let emotions control the player.

So, yes there will be big points as long as emotions are in tennis.

A Questionable Call Should Cost Only One Point

Questionable line calls are intrinsic in tennis. Many times, how you handle those calls will determine the outcome of a match. I have had many players come off the court after a loss still complaining about a line call that happened in the first set as if that were the *only* point played in the entire match!

Most players have gotten what they think are suspicious calls. Once you have made sure of your opponent's call and made sure they will not give way to how you saw the ball, let it go. Far too often, tennis players will mentally replay that disputed call and carry it with them into the next point and too many times into the next game or two. If you let this happen to you, that call has not only won that questionable point but subsequent points for your opponent too.

It's not what is happening around you that matters; what matters is what's happening inside you. It doesn't matter that you received a questionable call, what matters is how you handle it. Do not allow it to fester inside your head. *Get it out of your head and get on with the match.*

Cheating is Fleeting

If you have to cheat to win a tennis match, then the good feeling winning gives you is momentary, because you know you won the match by cheating. That doesn't feel as good as knowing you won the match by playing better than the opposition.

This cheating could also come back to haunt you. The next time you play that rival, you won't be confident that you beat them before, because you know you used underhanded ways to defeat the rival.

Win or lose, play fair. Don't cheat them or yourself out of the good feeling of winning.

Titles—If You're Not Enough without Them Then You Won't be Enough with Them

That statement was made in the movie *Cool Runnings* by John Candy. His character was talking about being a good person long after the medals are given out. Let's use the same statement but substitute "titles" for "medals."

You see, we all aspire to be good tennis players. When striving for the goals we set, whether our goals are trophies, titles, money, or rankings, we must not lose sight of the fact that tennis is what we do, *not who we are*. Many tennis players, as they become better competitors, become so single-minded that they forget to be good people. They feel, "People will like and respect me because I'm good at what I do." In reality, people may *admire* you as a tennis player, some will even try to emulate you, but not many will *respect* you as a person. You will be a person long after your glory days of tennis are over.

Will Beats Skill

In any sport, it's not good enough just to have the skill (talent) to play the game. By skill, I mean the ability to play the game at a high level of proficiency. But as the saying goes, "Talent means you're not there yet." There are many talented athletes in all sports who never reach their full potential because they think that being skillful will get them through to the next level. This may be true up to a certain level of play but eventually the skillful participant will often lose to less skillful opponents. Tennis is a prime example. As a matter of record, players of less skill can beat skillful players, because of their will to win.

Being skilled in tennis doesn't give you an excuse to sit back and rest on your talent. You have to possess another ingredient to help you achieve your full potential. That ingredient is will.

The will to:

learn more,

do more,

sacrifice more,

commit more, and

give whatever it takes to achieve your goal(s).

Wouldn't it be dreadful to look back at your playing days and realize the skill and talent was there but your will wasn't? I guarantee if that happens to you, you will wonder *what if* for the rest of your life. You can't get the what ifs back. Don't die wondering.

I want to leave you, the reader, with this one last thought. When you're playing a match, and momentum, net cords, and line calls are not going your way, think of the following:

The Competitive Spirit

*"Strength does not come from winning. Your struggles develop your strengths. When you go through hardships and decide **not** to surrender, that is strength"*

-Unknown

About the Author

Curly Davis's hometown is Louisville, Kentucky, where he has lived most of his life. As a junior he was the Kentucky State Junior Champion and also held numerous other titles.

He went on the pro circuit but knew that teaching the sport was his passion. Curly started teaching tennis in 1968 in the Louisville, Kentucky, public parks system. It was through this experience that he realized that teaching tennis was all he wanted to do.

In those early days of teaching, Curly developed a unique teaching style that has brought him local and national recognition. He has had numerous articles published in various tennis publications. Other honors include the Kentucky Tennis Association's 2009 Pro of the Year; induction in the Kentucky Tennis Hall of Fame; the Southern Professional Tennis Association's Kentucky Pro of the Year in 1985 and 1987; WDNG radio station's Citizen of the Day. Curly was selected by the United States Tennis Association as one of twenty-four coaches in the US to attend High Performance Coaches Workshops because of his successful work with high-performance tennis athletes.

Curly is a member of the United States Professional Tennis Association (USPTA) and a lifetime member of United States Tennis Association (USTA). He is a member of the Kentucky Tennis Association (KTA), where he held many offices, including president and vice president, Southern Tennis Association, (STA) where he was vice chair of the Junior Tennis Council & Player Development.

Curly directs his tennis camp, located in Naples, Florida, where he teaches players of all levels and ages. His web-site is www.curlydavistennis.com

Made in the USA
Lexington, KY
23 September 2016